GCSE History is always topical with CGP...

If you're studying "Anglo-Saxon and Norman England, c1060-88" for Edexcel GCSE History, this CGP Topic Guide is packed with more helpful info than the Domesday Book.

It has crystal-clear notes for the whole topic, plenty of activities, sample answers, exam tips and exam-style questions. It'd be good enough to eat if the Earls weren't revolting...

How to access your free Online Edition

This book includes a free Online Edition to read on your PC, Mac or tablet. To access it, just go to **cgpbooks.co.uk/extras** and enter this code...

3432 6708 6301 0995

By the way, this code only works for one person. If somebody else has used this book before you, they might have already claimed the Online Edition.

CGP — still the best! ☺

Our sole aim here at CGP is to produce the highest quality books — carefully written, immaculately presented and dangerously close to being funny.

Then we work our socks off to get them out to you — at the cheapest possible prices.

Published by CGP

Editors: Andy Cashmore, Sophie Herring, Catherine Heygate and Jack Tooth.

Contributor: Paddy Gannon.

With thanks to Emma Cleasby, Sarah Elsdon, Catherine Heygate and Helen Tanner for the proofreading.
With thanks to Emily Smith for the copyright research.

Acknowledgements:
Cover Image: The Battle of Hastings, English School, (20th century) / Private Collection / © Look and Learn / Bridgeman Images.
Image of King Cnut and Queen Emma on page 6 from The British Library, Stowe MS 944, f.6, New Minster Liber Vitae.
With thanks to Mary Evans for permission to use the images on pages 22, 24, 30 and 44.
With thanks to Alamy for permission to use the image on page 36.
Image used on page 38: Robert wounding his father, King William I, January 1079, from A Chronicle of England BC 55 to AD 1485, pub. London, 1863 (colour litho), Doyle, James William Edmund (1822-92) / Private Collection / The Stapleton Collection / Bridgeman Images.
Image used on page 46: © Oliver-Bonjoch. Licensed under the Creative Commons Attribution-Share Alike 2.0 Generic license.
https://creativecommons.org/licenses/by-sa/2.0/deed.en

ISBN: 978 1 78908 293 7
Printed by Elanders Ltd, Newcastle upon Tyne.
Clipart from Corel®

Based on the classic CGP style created by Richard Parsons.

Text, design, layout and original illustrations © Coordination Group Publications Ltd. (CGP) 2019
All rights reserved.

Photocopying more than 5% of this book is not permitted, even if you have a CLA licence.
Extra copies are available from CGP with next day delivery • 0800 1712 712 • www.cgpbooks.co.uk

Contents

Exam Skills

Exam Hints and Tips 2

Anglo-Saxon England and the Norman Conquest, 1060-1066

Anglo-Saxon Society and Government 4
Life in Anglo-Saxon England 6
The House of Godwin 8
Harold, Tostig and King Edward 10
Claimants to the Throne in 1066 12
The Struggle for the Throne 14
The Battle of Hastings 16
Worked Exam-Style Question 18
Exam-Style Questions 19

William I in Power: Securing the Kingdom, 1066-1087

William Becomes King of England 20
Norman Castles 22
The Design of Norman Castles 24
Resistance to Norman Rule, 1068-1069 26
The Harrying of the North 28
Resistance to Norman Rule, 1070-1071 30
The Revolt of the Earls 32
Worked Exam-Style Question 34
Exam-Style Questions 35

Norman England, 1066-1088

Norman Society 36
Norman Government 38
Life in Norman England 42
Domesday Book 44
Norman Culture 46
The Norman Church 48
Bishop Odo of Bayeux 50
William I and Robert Curthose 52
The Death of William I 54
Worked Exam-Style Question 56
Exam-Style Questions 58

Answers 59
Index 78

Exam Hints and Tips

You'll have to take three papers in Edexcel GCSE History. This book will help you with Paper 2, Booklet B.

You will take 3 Papers altogether

1) Paper 1 is 1 hour 15 minutes long. It's worth 52 marks — 30% of your GCSE. This paper will be divided into 2 sections:
   - Section A: Historic Environment.
   - Section B: Thematic Study.

It's really important that you make sure you know which topics you're studying for each paper.

2) Paper 2 is 1 hour 45 minutes long. It's worth 64 marks — 40% of your GCSE. This paper will be divided into two question and answer booklets:
   - Booklet P: Period Study.
   - Booklet B: British Depth Study.

This book covers the British Depth Study Anglo-Saxon and Norman England, c1060-88.

3) Paper 3 is 1 hour 20 minutes long. It's worth 52 marks — 30% of your GCSE. This paper will be divided into 2 sections, both about a Modern Depth Study:
   - Section A: 2 questions, one of which is based on a source.
   - Section B: A four-part question based on 2 sources and 2 interpretations.

Remember these Tips for Approaching the Questions

Organise your Time in the exam

1) In the exam, you'll have to answer three questions on Anglo-Saxon and Norman England and three questions on your Period Study. It's important to stay organised so that you have time to answer all the questions.
2) The more marks a question is worth, the longer your answer should be.
3) Don't get carried away writing lots for a question that's only worth 4 marks — you'll need to leave time for the higher mark questions.

Try to leave a few minutes at the end of the exam to go back and read over your answers.

Always use a Clear Writing Style

1) Start a new paragraph for each new point you want to discuss.
2) Try to use clear handwriting and pay attention to spelling, grammar and punctuation.

Stay Focused on the question

1) Make sure that you answer the question. Don't just chuck in everything you know about the topic.
2) Think about what the key words are in the question. For longer questions, it's a good idea to scribble down a quick plan of your main points before you start writing. Cross through this neatly at the end so it isn't marked.
3) Your answers have got to be relevant and accurate — make sure you include precise details like the dates of battles and rebellions and the names of the people involved in them.

It might help to write the first sentence of every paragraph in a way that addresses the question, e.g. "Another reason why the Normans won the Battle of Hastings was..."

Exam Skills

Exam Hints and Tips

This page is all about the British Depth Study. There are three questions which test two main skills.

There are Three exam questions in the British Depth Study

1) The first question will ask you to describe two features of something — it might be an event, a group of people or another significant aspect from the period.

2) In the next question, you'll be asked to explain the causes of a specific event or development.

3) Finally, you'll need to answer one more question, from a choice of two. Each will give you a statement and you'll be asked how far you agree with it.

4) In question types 2) and 3), you'll be given some 'stimulus points' — hints about things you could include in your answer. You don't have to include details about these stimulus points, so don't panic if you can't remember much about them. Even if you do write about the stimulus points, you must add other information too — if you don't, you can't get full marks.

> Describe two features of local government in Anglo-Saxon England. [4 marks]

> Explain why the English Church was reformed under William I. [12 marks]

> 'The Norman Conquest had little impact on English society and culture.' How far do you agree? Explain your answer. [16 marks]

The British Depth Study tests Two Main Skills

Knowledge and Understanding

1) For all the British Depth Study questions, you'll get marks for showing knowledge and understanding of the key features of the topic.

2) You'll need to use accurate and relevant information to support your answers in the exam.

> The Knowledge and Understanding activities in this book will help you to revise the important facts about the period so that you have plenty of information to help you in the exam.

Thinking Historically

1) As well as knowing the facts about Anglo-Saxon and Norman England, you'll also need to use historical concepts to analyse key events and developments. These concepts include significance, continuity and change, and cause and consequence.

2) You'll need to be able to find links between different events and explain why things happened the way they did.

3) You'll also need to use historical concepts to give a judgement on an issue. This may require you to explain how important you think a person, event or development was in Anglo-Saxon and Norman England. You should do this by weighing up how important the topic in the question is against other factors.

> The Thinking Historically activities will help you understand the causes and consequences of different events, similarities and differences within the periods, and how far things changed or stayed the same in Anglo-Saxon and Norman England.

EXAM TIP — *An exam about Norman England? It's positively medieval...*
These pages might seem like an awful lot to take in, but don't worry — this book is crammed with helpful questions and activities to help you practise all the skills you need for the exam.

Exam Skills

Anglo-Saxon Society and Government

To understand the impact of the Norman Conquest, you need to know what England was like before 1066.

The King was at the Top of the Hierarchy

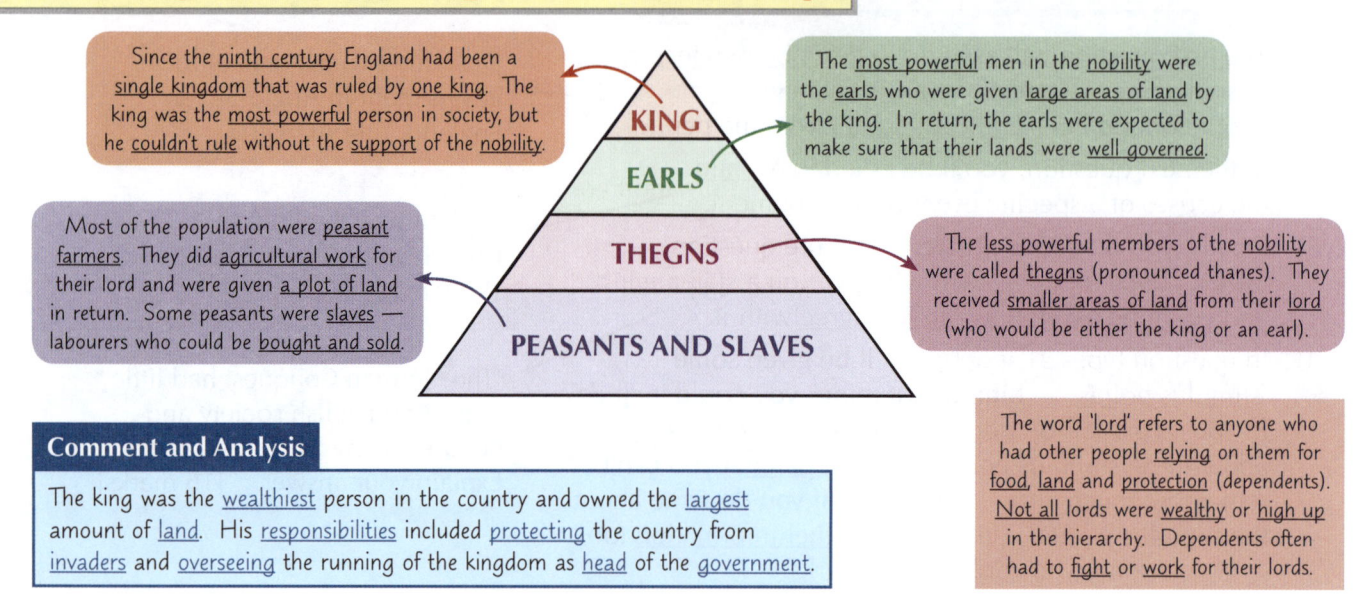

Since the ninth century, England had been a single kingdom that was ruled by one king. The king was the most powerful person in society, but he couldn't rule without the support of the nobility.

Pyramid: KING / EARLS / THEGNS / PEASANTS AND SLAVES

The most powerful men in the nobility were the earls, who were given large areas of land by the king. In return, the earls were expected to make sure that their lands were well governed.

Most of the population were peasant farmers. They did agricultural work for their lord and were given a plot of land in return. Some peasants were slaves — labourers who could be bought and sold.

The less powerful members of the nobility were called thegns (pronounced thanes). They received smaller areas of land from their lord (who would be either the king or an earl).

Comment and Analysis

The king was the wealthiest person in the country and owned the largest amount of land. His responsibilities included protecting the country from invaders and overseeing the running of the kingdom as head of the government.

The word 'lord' refers to anyone who had other people relying on them for food, land and protection (dependents). Not all lords were wealthy or high up in the hierarchy. Dependents often had to fight or work for their lords.

The system of government was Sophisticated and Organised

1) The king ruled the country supported by the king's council, also known as the Witan. This was a group of the most powerful nobles in the country, as well as high-ranking churchmen (e.g. bishops, see p.6). They advised the king and helped him to govern.

2) Churchmen played a key role in government. They could read and write, so the king used them to create all the written records that were needed to manage the kingdom.

3) Additionally, the king appointed earls and sheriffs to help him to govern the country:

- An earl was responsible for overseeing the government in his own earldom. An earldom typically covered a large area of land, giving the earl access to a lot of wealth and power.
- The earldoms were divided into shires (a bit like modern counties). A shire-reeve, or sheriff (who was usually a thegn), controlled the government within each shire.
- The shires were divided up into smaller areas called hundreds. These were made up of multiple villages, and were also controlled by the sheriffs and their deputies.

4) When the king summoned a region's fighting forces (the fyrd, see p.14), the earls and lower nobility were responsible for organising the troops and leading them into battle.

5) The earls and sheriffs made sure taxes were collected. The Anglo-Saxon tax system was highly organised — the amount of tax owed by each shire was based on the value of its land, and taxes were paid in cash.

Earls and Sheriffs enforced Law and Order

1) Another important responsibility for earls and sheriffs was to run local courts and bring criminals to justice.

2) The shire courts tried criminal cases and dealt with cases involving land and property. These courts were overseen by an earl and attended by important people in the shire like major landowners and churchmen.

3) For less serious crimes, like failing to repay small debts or stealing livestock, there were other courts known as hundred courts. These were overseen by a sheriff or his deputies.

4) The punishments used ranged from a fine to the death penalty, depending on the seriousness of the crime.

Anglo-Saxon Society and Government

There's a lot of information on the previous page about Anglo-Saxon society and government. Have a go at these activities to practise what you've learnt and to make sure everything you've read has really sunk in.

Knowledge and Understanding

The diagram below shows the social hierarchy in Anglo-Saxon England.

1) Copy and complete the diagram, stating what sort of people were at each level in the hierarchy and adding as much extra information about the people at this level as you can.

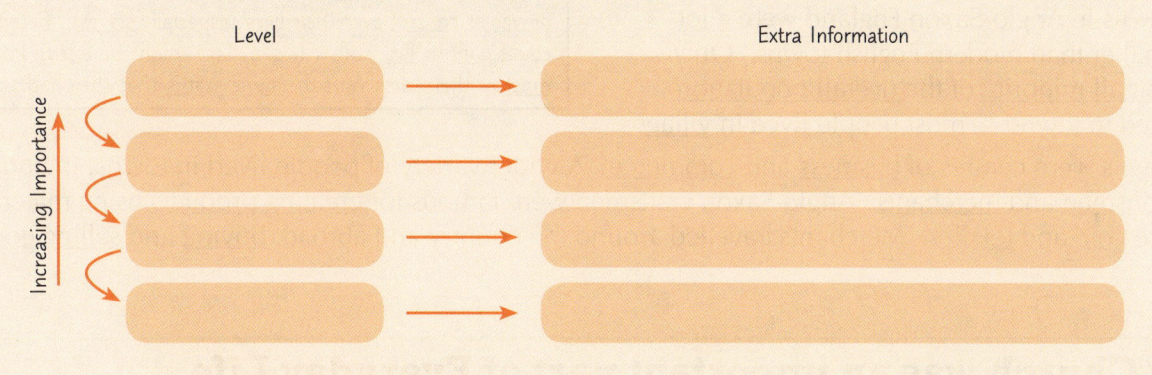

   Level → Extra Information (Increasing Importance)

2) Explain why churchmen were important to Anglo-Saxon government.

3) Use the information on the previous page to write a definition for each of the following terms:

   a) Witan   b) Shire   c) Hundred

4) Copy and complete the mind map below, giving examples which show that the Anglo-Saxon government was sophisticated and organised. You should include as much detail as possible.

   Anglo-Saxon government

5) In your own words, explain the responsibilities of sheriffs and earls in Anglo-Saxon England. Include the following key words in your answer:

   fyrd   taxes   courts

EXAM TIP

I didn't realise the Anglo-Saxons made pyramids as well...
You need to know specific details for the four-mark question in the exam — to get full marks, you'll have to describe two features of a topic and give relevant supporting information.

Anglo-Saxon England and the Norman Conquest, 1060-1066

Life in Anglo-Saxon England

The lives of ordinary Anglo-Saxons mostly involved farming and going to church... sounds exciting, doesn't it?

England's Economy relied on Agriculture

1) The vast majority of people in Anglo-Saxon England were peasants or slaves. They lived in villages, which were governed by a thegn. Farming was vital to a village's economy, so peasants and slaves mostly worked the land.

2) Towns in Anglo-Saxon England were a lot smaller than modern English towns. Only a small minority of the overall population lived in towns — most people lived in villages.

3) Towns were centres of business and commerce. A wider variety of people lived in towns, including craftsmen and merchants. Anglo-Saxon craftsmen were famous for creating products using materials like gold and textiles. Merchants travelled around the country and abroad, buying and selling goods.

Comment and Analysis

People's lives were shaped by their social status. Those near the top of the social hierarchy could become wealthy and influential. Those nearer the bottom were often poor and didn't have much power or control over their lives (especially slaves). People could gain or lose status (e.g. a slave might be freed), but most of them died with the same status that they had at birth.

The Church was an important part of Everyday Life

1) Before 1066, the Church played an important role in Anglo-Saxon society and its influence over ordinary people was already growing.

2) The Anglo-Saxon Church was split up into sixteen large areas called dioceses, each one controlled by a bishop. By 1066, these regions were starting to be divided into smaller areas called parishes.

3) Each parish was based around a local community, so the Church became more involved in ordinary people's lives.

4) Parish churches were built in towns and villages — each church had a priest to look after the people in the parish.

The priest said mass regularly and performed key ceremonies such as baptism and burial. He also got people to confess their sins and do penance (show that they're sorry for their sins).

The Church and the Nobility had an Important Relationship

1) The Church held influence over the nobility, as well as over ordinary people.

2) The king and his nobles gave churches gifts of land and precious objects, and helped to protect them from violence and robbery. This was called patronage.

3) The nobility sometimes sent their second-born sons to train as priests, which helped the Church to grow. This also reduced competition for land within the nobility by giving some men a job within the Church.

4) Nobles tried to control the appointment of bishops, abbots and priests so that they could give these valuable, influential posts to their relatives and followers.

5) In return, churchmen prayed for their patrons. Prayer was important to the nobility, because they believed that it would give them success on earth and help them to get into heaven.

6) Even the king needed the Church's support to legitimise his claim to power — people thought that a ruler needed God's support to be successful. If the Church supported him, it was seen as a sign that God was on his side.

Comment and Analysis

The sources produced by churchmen were often influenced by the relationship between the Church and the nobility — for example, this image shows King Cnut (a Danish king who ruled England in the early 11th century) being crowned by an angel. It was created by the monks of Winchester, who were close to the king. It makes his claim to the throne seem more legitimate (valid), as it implies that God wants him to be king.

Anglo-Saxon England and the Norman Conquest, 1060-1066

Life in Anglo-Saxon England

The activities on this page will help you to understand the ins and outs of life in Anglo-Saxon England.

Knowledge and Understanding

1) Copy and complete the table below by listing different features of villages and towns in Anglo-Saxon England. Add as many rows as you need.

Villages	Towns

2) In Anglo-Saxon England, people's lives were shaped by their place in the social hierarchy. How was life different for people at the top of the hierarchy compared to people at the bottom of the hierarchy?

3) Explain how the Anglo-Saxon Church was structured.

4) Give two examples of how the Church was involved in ordinary people's lives.

Thinking Historically

In Anglo-Saxon England, the Church and the nobility both benefited from their relationship.

1) Copy and complete the mind maps below, giving as many ways as possible that the Church and the nobility benefited from their relationship with each other.

   ← Church →   ← Nobility →
        ↓   ↓

2) Do you think the nobility or the Church was more important in helping the king govern the country? Give reasons for your answer, using the information on pages 4 and 6 to help.

Life in Anglo-Saxon England — eat, sleep, work, repeat...
It's really important to understand change and continuity during the period you're studying. By learning about Anglo-Saxon England, you'll be able to compare it to Norman England later on.

Anglo-Saxon England and the Norman Conquest, 1060-1066

The House of Godwin

Edward the Confessor was King of England from 1042 to 1066, but he didn't have complete authority — people like Godwin, Earl of Wessex, and his children had a say in the running of the kingdom too.

Godwin was one of the Most Powerful Men in England

1) As the son of a thegn (see p.4), Godwin was born into the lower nobility. However, he was a clever man and a skilled politician, and worked his way up to an earldom. In 1018, Godwin became the Earl of Wessex — an earldom in the south, which was the oldest and richest in the whole kingdom.

2) In 1042, Godwin backed Edward's claim to the throne — a few years later, Edward married Godwin's daughter (Edith). This added to Godwin's power and influence.

3) However, Godwin became less powerful as the king started to favour the Normans in the royal household.

4) In 1051, Godwin rebelled unsuccessfully against Edward and was outlawed by the king. He and his family fled the country.

5) In 1052, Godwin returned to England with a large army and demanded to be restored as Earl of Wessex. Edward didn't have enough support to fight him, so accepted his demands.

Comment and Analysis

Edward's mother was from Normandy, and he had spent over twenty years in exile there while England was ruled by Scandinavians (1013-1042). After he became king, Edward installed the Norman supporters that he'd gained in positions of power in England. Many English nobles, including Godwin, resented this foreign influence.

Edward ordered Godwin to punish the town of Dover after a fight between the townspeople and a visiting French nobleman. Godwin refused. He gathered an army and went to confront the king, but didn't have enough men to overpower the king's forces.

Harold Godwinson became Earl of Wessex after Godwin's Death

1) Godwin's son Harold was Earl of East Anglia. This made Harold very wealthy and gave him experience as a military leader, because he had to defend the lands in his earldom.

2) When Godwin died in 1053, Harold gave up the earldom of East Anglia to become Earl of Wessex. This made him the most powerful man in the country after the king.

3) Harold had strong relations with important churchmen, making his position more secure. These included Stigand — Bishop of Winchester and Archbishop of Canterbury (see p.48).

4) Harold played an important role in governing the country. Edward knew he couldn't rule without the support of the nobility (see p.4), so had to work with earls like Harold. As the king got older, Harold became more and more responsible for helping to run the kingdom.

The Godwins Dominated English Politics

1) Harold and his siblings were dominant figures in England in the final years of Edward's reign. His brothers (Tostig, Gyrth and Leofwine) were also earls, and his sister (Edith) was the queen.

Edith was sent to a nunnery after Godwin's rebellion (see above), but she returned as soon as he was reinstated as Earl of Wessex — this showed that the Godwins' power in the kingdom had been restored.

2) The Godwins controlled a large amount of land across the kingdom. Harold was Earl of Wessex and Tostig was Earl of Northumbria — two of the largest and most important earldoms in England.

Harold made sure that Tostig was made Earl of Northumbria rather than the earldom being given to a rival family. He wanted to strengthen his family's position and reduce the power of his rivals.

3) These lands made the Godwins very wealthy, helping them to acquire and maintain a large number of followers. They gained support from their allies by granting them land and other gifts, and paid skilled fighters to join their households.

4) The family had military power. In 1063, Harold and Tostig worked together in order to defeat a rebellious Welsh king.

Anglo-Saxon England and the Norman Conquest, 1060-1066

The House of Godwin

Now that you know all about the Godwins, you can use your knowledge to explain their impact on the government of Anglo-Saxon England. That's what the activities on this page are all about.

Knowledge and Understanding

1) Explain who each of the following people was:
   a) Edward
   b) Godwin
   c) Harold
   d) Tostig
   e) Edith
   f) Gyrth and Leofwine

2) Copy and complete the timeline below by filling in the key events for the Godwin family that happened in each year. Try to give as much detail as you can.

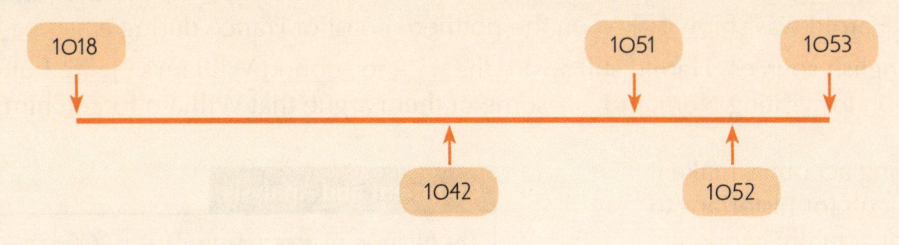

   1018 — 1042 — 1051 — 1052 — 1053

Thinking Historically

1) Copy and complete the mind map below, explaining why each of the factors in the green boxes helped to make the Godwins powerful in Anglo-Saxon England. You should include as much detail as possible.

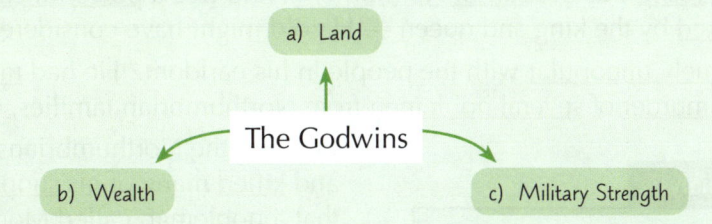

   The Godwins
   a) Land
   b) Wealth
   c) Military Strength

2) In the exam, you'll be asked to make a judgement about a statement. Give at least one piece of evidence for and one piece of evidence against each of the statements below.

   a) The Godwins became powerful because of Harold Godwinson.
   b) King Edward had a lot of power over the Godwins.
   c) Harold's relationship with important figures was the main reason why his power was secure.

EXAM TIP

Edward the Confessor was up to the earls in Godwins...
When you're making a judgement about a statement in the exam, make sure you analyse evidence for and against the statement — it'll help you to write a more balanced answer.

Anglo-Saxon England and the Norman Conquest, 1060-1066

Harold, Tostig and King Edward

King Edward was childless, so he had to name someone else as his successor. William, who was Duke of Normandy, believed the throne had been promised to him — but not everyone agreed...

Harold might have sworn an Oath to William of Normandy

1) Harold visited Normandy at some point in 1064 or 1065. He met with William, Duke of Normandy, and went on a military campaign with him. However, the actual reason for Harold's visit is unclear:

   - According to Norman sources, Harold had been sent by King Edward to name William as the next King of England — Harold supposedly swore an oath to support William's claim. However, these sources give conflicting information (e.g. when and where this happened).
   - According to some English sources, Harold went to secure the release of his brother and his nephew, who had been hostages in Normandy since 1051. However, others suggest Harold was shipwrecked on the northern coast of France during a fishing trip.
   - In the English sources, Harold still swore the oath to support William's claim, but it wasn't the reason for visiting Normandy — some of them argue that William forced him to do it.

2) These conflicting accounts make it extremely difficult for historians to figure out what actually happened. Most of the sources are also biased, so it's hard to tell if they're accurate.

3) Whether Harold swore the oath or not, the Normans used it to undermine his claim to the throne and justify the invasion in 1066.

Comment and Analysis

The Norman sources were made after 1066 to support William's claim to the throne. For example, the Bayeux Tapestry (see p.50) shows Harold swearing an oath to William, but it was William's half-brother who ordered the tapestry to be created. The English sources are also biased, but in a different way — they were made to present William as a invader who wrongfully seized the throne.

Harold sent Tostig into Exile

1) Harold's brother Tostig was the Earl of Northumbria. He was a powerful earl and a military leader who was well liked by the king and queen — Harold might have considered him a rival for power.

2) Tostig was extremely unpopular with the people in his earldom. He had raised taxes in the region and ordered the murder of several noblemen from Northumbrian families, who he saw as a threat.

Comment and Analysis

Tostig's exile left Harold in a strong position — it gained him new allies and removed a potential rival for the throne. Tostig even claimed Harold had conspired with the rebels to have him exiled. Whether this is true or not, his exile meant that Harold was undoubtedly the most powerful earl in England by the time Edward died.

3) In 1065, the Northumbrians rebelled against Tostig and killed many of his supporters. They demanded that a nobleman called Morcar was appointed earl.

4) King Edward tried to support Tostig, sending Harold to deal with the rebels. However, Harold agreed to appoint Morcar as earl and to send Tostig into exile. Tostig left the kingdom to live with his wife's family.

5) By helping Morcar to become Earl of Northumbria, Harold gained powerful allies in the north of the kingdom.

England faced a Succession Crisis when King Edward Died

1) Edward died in January 1066. He didn't have any children, so there was no clear successor to the throne.

2) Edward had been King of England since 1042. His father was the Anglo-Saxon king, Aethelred II. His mother was a daughter of the Duke of Normandy, and Edward had been raised in Normandy.

3) Between 1013 and 1042, England's kings included three Scandinavians — Swein, Cnut and Harthacnut.

4) Due to the close connections between England, Normandy and Scandinavia, there were people in all three regions who believed they had a strong claim to the throne.

Harold, Tostig and King Edward

There was a lot of uncertainty about who would succeed Edward as king after he died. The activities below will help you understand why this was the case and the impact that this uncertainty had on the succession.

Knowledge and Understanding

It's unclear what actually happened when Harold visited Normandy in 1064 or 1065.

1) Copy and complete the table below, explaining what information the Norman and English sources give about Harold's visit to Normandy.

Norman Sources	English Sources

2) Explain how the Norman sources supported William's claim to the throne.

3) Copy and complete the mind map below, giving the causes and main events of the rebellion against Tostig in 1065. Try to give as much detail as possible.

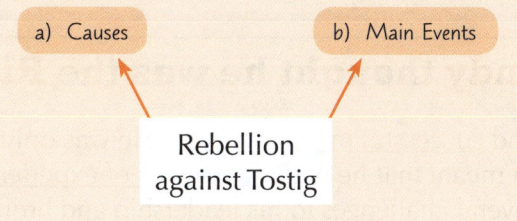

- a) Causes
- b) Main Events

→ Rebellion against Tostig

Thinking Historically

1) In your own words, explain why the rebellion against Tostig strengthened Harold's position in England.

2) Harold was in a strong position when King Edward died, but there were also other claimants to the throne of England. Explain why there were claimants to the throne in the following regions:

- a) Normandy
- b) Scandinavia

EXAM TIP

Harold's visit to Normandy is a real source of confusion...
If you're writing about the oath, it's good to mention the differences in the Norman and English sources. You won't be asked to analyse any sources for the Normans part of the exam, though.

Anglo-Saxon England and the Norman Conquest, 1060-1066

Claimants to the Throne in 1066

When King Edward died in 1066, there were a few different people who all had a claim to the empty throne...

There were Two Englishmen with a Claim to the Throne

1) At the start of 1066, Edgar Atheling and Harold Godwinson were both in a position to inherit the throne. However, Harold was in a much stronger position than Edgar.
2) Edgar Atheling was related to King Edward. However, Edgar was only a teenager and he hadn't proven himself as a leader, making it difficult for him to gain support from the Witan (see p.14).

> **Comment and Analysis**
>
> There were no fixed rules about succession, but being related to the king could strengthen your claim to the throne. However, even those with a strong claim also had to be able to use military force to take control of the country and show they would be an effective ruler.

3) Harold was the most powerful nobleman in England and he had experience of leading an army. He was close to the royal family — his father helped Edward to become king, and his sister was Edward's wife (see p.8). Harold claimed Edward had asked him to become king on his deathbed.
4) Harold was ambitious and believed that becoming king would secure his authority. In the past, powerful nobles had been viewed as a threat to royal authority, so a new king might have tried to reduce Harold's power in England. Harold could prevent this happening by taking the throne.

William of Normandy thought he was the Rightful Successor

1) William was a powerful and successful military leader. He was only a child when he became Duke of Normandy, which meant that he had many years of experience as a ruler. During this period, he had defeated several challenges to his leadership and brought stability to Normandy.
2) William was another distant relative of King Edward. According to some sources, Edward had promised the kingdom to William and Harold Godwinson had sworn to support him (see p.10).
3) William's claim was also supported by the Pope, which strengthened it by suggesting that God was on his side.
4) Becoming King of England would make William more powerful. As a duke, he was meant to serve and obey the King of France — if he took the throne of England, he would have the same high status as the French king.
5) Ruling England as well as Normandy would also make William much wealthier — England was a rich country with lots of precious metals and fertile land for farming.

Harold (right) swearing an oath to William (left).

Harald Hardrada wanted to Conquer England

1) Harald Hardrada was the King of Norway. He was another experienced ruler who was known for his military prowess. He claimed he was the true successor to the Scandinavian kings who had ruled England before Edward the Confessor.

> Hardrada wanted to reconquer the empire of King Cnut, who had ruled over Norway, Denmark and England earlier in the 11th century.

2) His claim was supported by Harold Godwinson's brother, Tostig. Harold had played a part in exiling Tostig in 1065 (see p.10). By supporting Hardrada, Tostig might have hoped to get revenge on his brother and reclaim his former earldom of Northumbria.

Anglo-Saxon England and the Norman Conquest, 1060-1066

# Claimants to the Throne in 1066

SKILLS PRACTICE

When you're writing about the events of 1066, there are lots of important names to get your head around. The activities on this page take a look at the most important figures in the struggle to become King of England.

Knowledge and Understanding

1) For each of the following claimants to the throne in 1066, explain who they were and why they wanted to be King of England.
   a) Harold Godwinson
   b) William of Normandy
   c) Harald Hardrada

2) In Anglo-Saxon England, there were no fixed rules about who would succeed to the throne when a king died. What factors were important in deciding who would be the next king?

Thinking Historically

1) Copy and complete the table below, explaining what you think the strengths and weaknesses of each person's claim to the throne were in 1066. Try to give as much detail as possible.

Claimant	Strengths	Weaknesses
a) Edgar Atheling		
b) Harold Godwinson		
c) William of Normandy		
d) Harald Hardrada		

2) Who do you think had the strongest claim to the throne in 1066? Explain your answer.

Use your table from question 1 to help you answer questions 2 and 3.

3) Explain who you think had the weakest claim to the throne in 1066.

EXAM TIP

An Englishman, a Norman and a Viking went into a war...

There's a lot of key information to learn about 1066 — make sure you know the order that events happened in, the names of all the important figures and the roles these people played.

Anglo-Saxon England and the Norman Conquest, 1060-1066

The Struggle for the Throne

Harold Godwinson was crowned King of England in January 1066. Unfortunately for Harold, his rival claimants weren't willing to give up without a fight, and he was forced to defend the throne.

Harold Godwinson became King after Edward Died

1) The Witan didn't hesitate to choose Harold as Edward's successor. He was crowned in Westminster Abbey on the same day that Edward was buried.

2) Harold's reign only lasted nine months. He spent most of it trying to secure his position as king and preparing to defend England against attacks from other claimants.

3) He tried to strengthen his support from important allies. He strengthened his alliance with Edwin, Earl of Mercia and Morcar, Earl of Northumbria by marrying their sister.

4) Harold was prepared for an invasion by mid-1066. Once he had been crowned king, he gathered his forces and prepared to defend the south coast in case the Normans invaded. Harold's army consisted of housecarls, who were highly trained professional warriors, and the fyrd — a part-time defensive force.

Comment and Analysis

When an Anglo-Saxon king died, the Witan could play a role in choosing his successor, especially if there was a dispute over who should rule. They knew foreign threats were likely after Edward's death, and agreed that Harold was the best leader to protect the country from invasion.

The fyrd was made up of ordinary men who had to leave their normal work and provide military service whenever the king summoned them. Members of the fyrd weren't professional fighters and they only served for two months at a time.

Harold Defeated the Scandinavian Invaders...

1) The Anglo-Saxons waited on the south coast throughout mid-1066, but nothing happened. By September, supplies were running low and Harold's men needed to return to their land to collect the harvest, so he dismissed the fyrd and returned to London.

2) Soon after Harold dismissed the fyrd, an army led by Harald Hardrada (see p.12) and supported by Tostig invaded north-eastern England. They moved down the coast, attacking towns and villages along the way.

3) Hardrada and Tostig's armies didn't encounter any major opposition until they moved inland towards York — the most important town in Northumbria. Harold's northern allies, Edwin and Morcar, gathered their own armies in an attempt to fight off the invaders.

4) These armies fought at the Battle of Gate Fulford on 20th September, and Edwin and Morcar were defeated. This victory meant Hardrada and Tostig had gained an important foothold in the north of England.

5) Harold raced north to face Hardrada. He had dismissed the fyrd, so he needed to gather troops on the way. He moved quickly and took Hardrada by surprise.

6) This gave Harold an advantage, and he defeated the invaders at the Battle of Stamford Bridge on 25th September. Hardrada and Tostig were both killed, along with huge numbers of their men. The remains of the Scandinavian army withdrew from England.

Earls Edwin and Morcar were younger and less knowledgeable than Harald Hardrada, who had many years of experience in battle. The Scandinavian army were fierce and skilled fighters compared to the less experienced Anglo-Saxon forces.

...but it left him Weak and Vulnerable to Attack

1) The Battle of Stamford Bridge was an important victory for Harold. He had defeated a powerful Scandinavian army and removed one of the main threats to the kingdom.

2) However, many of Harold's troops were killed in the battle and the rest were tired from marching and fighting. Harold had taken his forces a long way north to fight Hardrada and Tostig. This meant that the south coast was undefended and vulnerable to invasion.

3) When the Normans arrived in England a couple of days after the battle, Harold was at a disadvantage.

Anglo-Saxon England and the Norman Conquest, 1060-1066

The Struggle for the Throne

SKILLS PRACTICE

The Battle of Gate Fulford and the Battle of Stamford Bridge were hugely important events in Harold's short reign. These activities will get you thinking about the impact of them in more detail.

Knowledge and Understanding

1) Write a definition for each of the following terms:

   a) Fyrd   b) Housecarl

2) After Edward's death, the Witan were worried about foreign attacks on England. How did this influence the Witan's decision in choosing Edward's successor?

3) Harold was only King of England for nine months, but a lot of important events took place during his reign. Copy and complete the timeline below by filling in the events that happened at each point. Try to give as much detail as possible.

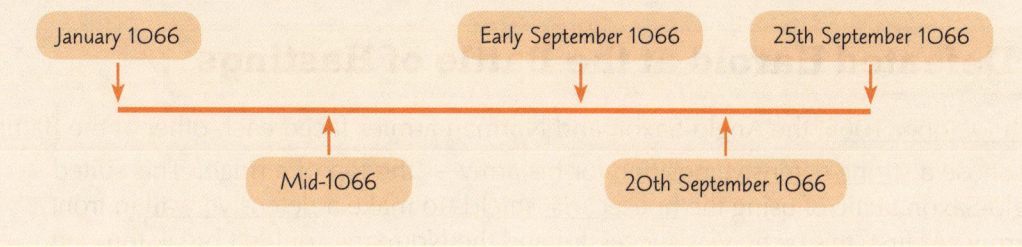

   January 1066 — Early September 1066 — 25th September 1066

   Mid-1066 — 20th September 1066

Thinking Historically

1) Copy and complete the table below, stating whether the Anglo-Saxons won or lost each battle and explaining why this was the outcome. Give as much detail as possible.

Battle	Did the Anglo-Saxons win or lose?	Explanation for outcome
a) Gate Fulford		
b) Stamford Bridge		

2) Why was the Battle of Stamford Bridge so significant for Harold? Explain your answer, thinking about the positive and negative consequences of the battle.

EXAM TIP

It's like a game of musical chairs, only a lot more violent...

In the exam, you'll need to use correct terminology (e.g. the fyrd) in your answer. This is a good way of showing the examiner that you really understand the topic you're writing about.

Anglo-Saxon England and the Norman Conquest, 1060-1066

The Battle of Hastings

The Norman and Anglo-Saxon armies faced each other at Hastings in October 1066 for one of the most famous battles in English history. Harold's defeat marked the end of the Anglo-Saxon period in England.

The Normans landed on the South Coast of England...

1) The Normans landed at Pevensey on 28th September, and started pillaging (raiding and stealing from) Harold's lands.

> William's forces were ready in August, but he needed to delay the invasion until September as the English Channel could only be crossed in good conditions. This delay might also have been a strategic decision — one historian has argued that William knew about Hardrada's invasion (see p.14), so didn't set sail until Harold had moved north, leaving the south coast undefended.

2) William's arrival forced Harold to hurry south to try to drive the Normans out. He spent a few days in London, but it wasn't enough to recover from the march and the Battle of Stamford Bridge, or to gather all of his troops.

3) Harold's army was weakened and exhausted, and the Norman army was much fresher in comparison. This gave the Normans a major advantage.

...and Defeated Harold at the Battle of Hastings

1) On 14th October 1066, the Anglo-Saxon and Norman armies faced each other at the Battle of Hastings.

2) Harold chose a strong defensive position for his army — the top of a ridge. This suited the Anglo-Saxon tactic of using the housecarls' shields to make a defensive wall in front of the army. At first, this tactic was successful and the Normans couldn't break through.

3) However, the Normans' tactics eventually broke the Anglo-Saxon shield wall:

- Part of the Norman army used a tactic called feigned flight — they pretended to run away. Some of the Anglo-Saxon army left their position to follow them.
- This weakened the Anglo-Saxons' defences, as the shield wall relied on everyone holding their position in the line. Once the shield wall was broken, the Norman cavalry (horsemen) could ride through and kill many of the Anglo-Saxon fighters.
- Harold was killed (possibly by a Norman arrow) — his brothers and allies Gyrth and Leofwine were also killed in the battle. The Anglo-Saxon army was defeated.

There are Different Reasons why the Normans Won

1) William and Harold were both experienced military leaders. However, Harold's decision to rush into battle probably contributed to his defeat. If he had waited, his troops would have been able to rest and his allies would have brought reinforcements. Harold also failed to keep control of his troops during the battle due to William's use of tactics (see above).

> Chance was also a factor in the Normans' victory — it was good luck for William that he was able to cross the Channel soon after Hardrada's invasion.

2) The Norman army was strong and well equipped. It was made up of a mixture of foot-soldiers, archers and cavalry. The archers were particularly effective — they were able to attack from a distance, meaning they could weaken the Anglo-Saxon shield wall without risking themselves.

3) The cavalry was also an important part of the Norman army. The riders were highly skilled and disciplined, and fighting on horseback allowed them to attack with greater speed and strength.

4) Harold had a traditional Anglo-Saxon army where all the troops fought on foot. His army also contained the fyrd (see p.14), who were much less experienced and disciplined than the professional Norman army they were fighting. Many of Harold's skilled fighters (the housecarls) had been killed at Stamford Bridge.

Anglo-Saxon England and the Norman Conquest, 1060-1066

The Battle of Hastings

The Battle of Hastings was a total disaster for Harold and the Anglo-Saxons, but a huge victory for William's Norman army. These activities will test your knowledge of the factors that decided the outcome of the battle.

Knowledge and Understanding

1) The Normans were ready to invade England in August 1066, but William delayed the invasion until September. Give two possible reasons for this.

2) In your own words, explain why the timing of the Normans' arrival gave them a major advantage over the Anglo-Saxons.

3) The flowchart below shows the main events of the Battle of Hastings. Copy and complete the flowchart by adding the missing information.

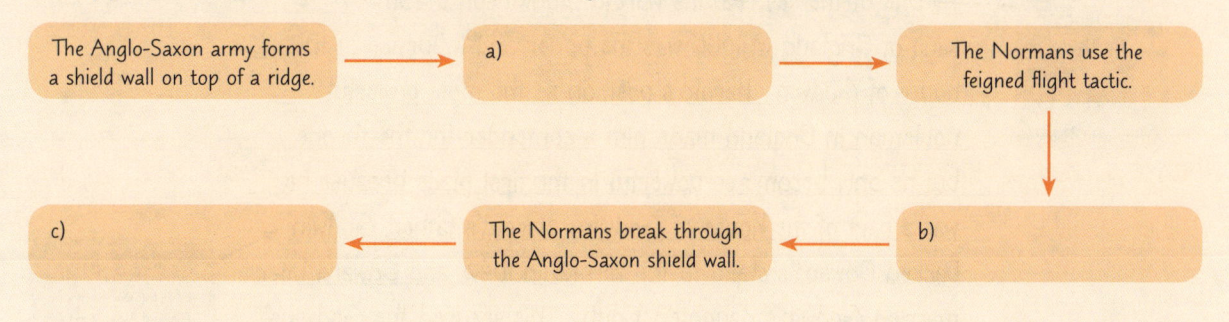

The Anglo-Saxon army forms a shield wall on top of a ridge. → a) → The Normans use the feigned flight tactic. → b) → The Normans break through the Anglo-Saxon shield wall. → c)

Thinking Historically

1) Copy and complete the table below, listing the similarities and differences between the Anglo-Saxon army and the Norman army at the Battle of Hastings. Give as much detail as possible.

Similarities	Differences

2) Do you think William's leadership or Harold's mistakes had more of an impact on the outcome of the Battle of Hastings? Explain your answer.

EXAM TIP

I'm quivering at the idea of getting shot with an arrow...

For the longer questions in the exam, it's important to take a few minutes to plan out your answer. This will help you to make sure that each of your points is answering the question.

Anglo-Saxon England and the Norman Conquest, 1060-1066

Worked Exam-Style Question

This page will help give you an idea of what you need to do to answer the 12-mark question in the exam.

Explain why Harold Godwinson became King of England in 1066.

You could mention:
- the house of Godwin
- Edward the Confessor

You should also use your own knowledge. [12 marks]

The prompts in the question are only there as a guide. To get a high mark, you'll also need to include ideas of your own that go beyond the prompts.

The first sentence in this paragraph links back to the question.

One of the key reasons Harold Godwinson became King of England in 1066 was the power and influence of the house of Godwin. Harold's position as the most powerful nobleman in England made him a contender for the throne, but he only became so powerful in the first place because he was a part of the house of Godwin. Harold's father, Godwin, backed Edward's claim to the throne in 1042, and Edward later married Godwin's daughter, Edith. This secured the Godwins' high status in England and allowed the family to prosper. Then, when Godwin died in 1053, Harold took over his earldom of Wessex. Controlling Wessex allowed Harold to demonstrate his strength and ability as a ruler, meaning he was a strong candidate for the throne. The power and influence gained by Godwin paved the way for Harold to become the most powerful nobleman in the country and eventually the King of England.

Including details like dates shows that you can provide accurate information.

This links the paragraph back to the question by explaining how this factor led to Harold becoming King of England.

It's important to include factors that weren't mentioned as prompts in the question.

Another reason why Harold Godwinson became King of England in 1066 was the influence of the Witan. After Edward's death, the Witan helped to choose his successor because there was no clear heir to the throne. The Witan was concerned that foreign rulers who had a claim to the throne, such as Harald Hardrada and William of Normandy, would see Edward's death as an opportunity to invade England. As a result, they wanted to pick a strong leader who could protect the country from invasion. Harold had more military experience than the other English claimant to the throne, Edgar Atheling, who was only in his teens. The Witan's concerns about a foreign threat therefore encouraged them to choose Harold as the next King of England in 1066.

Give specific examples to show how well you know the topic.

This is a shortened example — in the exam, you'll need to write about at least one more factor.

Anglo-Saxon England and the Norman Conquest, 1060-1066

Exam-Style Questions

This page will help you to practise the type of questions you'll be asked in the exam. For the longer 12-mark and 16-mark questions, remember to make a rough plan before you start writing your answers.

Exam-Style Questions

1) Describe two aspects of the legal system in Anglo-Saxon England.   [4 marks]

2) Explain why there was a succession crisis in England when King Edward died.

   You could mention:
   - Normandy
   - Scandinavia

   You should also use your own knowledge.   [12 marks]

3) 'The main reason William won the Battle of Hastings was his use of cavalry.'

   To what extent do you agree with this statement? Explain your answer.

   You could mention:
   - the fyrd
   - feigned flight

   You should also use your own knowledge.   [16 marks]

Anglo-Saxon England and the Norman Conquest, 1060-1066

William I in Power: Securing the Kingdom, 1066-1087

William Becomes King of England

William of Normandy defeated his main rival, Harold Godwinson, at the Battle of Hastings, but he wasn't king yet. The hard work of getting the kingdom under control was only just starting...

William was crowned King in December 1066

1) Although William had won the Battle of Hastings, the Anglo-Saxons didn't recognise him as king. A group of powerful nobles, including the Earls of Mercia and Northumbria (Edwin and Morcar), took refuge in London with Edgar Atheling (see p.12). They claimed Edgar was the rightful king.
2) Over the next two months, William seized control of south-eastern England and prepared to attack London. The Anglo-Saxons were unable to gather a strong enough army to fight back.
3) In December, the Anglo-Saxon nobles (including Edwin, Morcar and Edgar) met with William and surrendered to him, promising to remain loyal. This event is known as the submission of the earls.
4) On 25th December 1066, William was crowned King of England at Westminster Abbey in London.

The Anglo-Saxons weren't the only threat to William's rule — he was surrounded by hostile forces:
- The Welsh and the Scottish gave refuge and support to any Anglo-Saxon opposition.
- Harold Godwinson's sons were in exile in Ireland and launched attacks from there.
- The Danish kings still believed that they had a claim to the English throne (but they were too busy trying to keep Denmark under control to launch a bid for the throne).

William tried to satisfy the Normans and the Anglo-Saxons

After he became king, William tried to create a mixed Anglo-Norman nobility, which would include both Norman settlers and surviving members of the Anglo-Saxon elite.

1) William seized the land of Anglo-Saxon nobles who had died at Hastings or refused to accept him as king, but he allowed nobles who accepted his rule to keep their land.
2) William gave out the land he'd seized to the Normans who had helped him to become king, but there wasn't enough unoccupied land to satisfy all of them.
3) Some Norman settlers resorted to seizing land that belonged to surviving Anglo-Saxon nobles. This led to resentment, motivating many of the revolts that broke out at the start of William's reign (see p.26).

Comment and Analysis

William hoped to carry on in the style of Edward's reign, so that he would be seen as the true successor to Edward. At the start of his reign, he tried to keep as many Anglo-Saxon nobles in power as possible.

Norman settlement in England was important in helping William to establish authority, as it made sure he would always have loyal fighters on hand when he needed them.

The Marcher Earldoms helped to control the Welsh Border

1) When William conquered England, Wales was still an independent country. There was a risk that the Welsh might provide support and refuge to Anglo-Saxon rebels or cross the border to invade England.
2) William didn't have the military or financial resources to control the Welsh Marches on his own. He appointed earls to do it for him by creating the Marcher earldoms (Chester, Shrewsbury and Hereford).
3) William gave the Marcher earldoms to some of his closest allies, like Roger of Montgomery and William FitzOsbern, because he trusted them to deal with the threat of Welsh invasion.
4) In return for their extra responsibilities, the Marcher earls received privileges such as not paying tax and having permission to build as many castles as they liked. This made them very powerful.

The Welsh Marches (another name for the border between England and Wales) were an unstable area — before 1066, the Welsh and the Anglo-Saxons had come into conflict over the lands there.

William Becomes King of England

These activities will help you understand the challenges William faced once he became King of England.

Knowledge and Understanding

1) Copy and complete the timeline below by filling in the key events that led to William being crowned King of England. You can use the information on pages 16 and 20 to help you. Give as much detail as possible for each date.

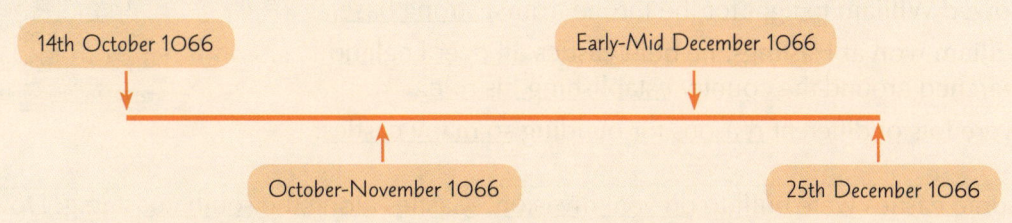

   - 14th October 1066
   - October-November 1066
   - Early-Mid December 1066
   - 25th December 1066

2) Copy and complete the table, explaining how each of the following nations was a threat to William's rule.

Nation	How they were a threat
a) Scotland	
b) Ireland	
c) Denmark	

Thinking Historically

1) Copy and complete the diagram below, explaining how each of the following helped William to establish control in England. Give as much detail as possible.

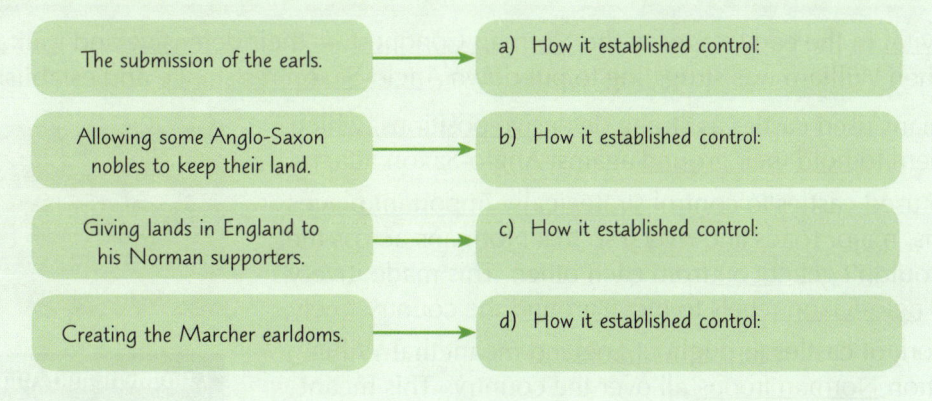

   - The submission of the earls. → a) How it established control:
   - Allowing some Anglo-Saxon nobles to keep their land. → b) How it established control:
   - Giving lands in England to his Norman supporters. → c) How it established control:
   - Creating the Marcher earldoms. → d) How it established control:

EXAM TIP

Dividing up the land was a royal mess...

It's important that you can use language to link an event to its causes and consequences — linking words and phrases like 'as a result', 'despite this', and 'therefore' can help you do this.

William I in Power: Securing the Kingdom, 1066-1087

Norman Castles

The Anglo-Saxons didn't really build castles, but the Normans were big fans of them — they built castles all over England after the conquest, and these were an important tool in helping William to maintain his power.

The Normans built lots of Castles throughout England

1) When the Normans landed at Pevensey in 1066, they immediately started building a castle — they also built one in Hastings before the battle there. This allowed William to fight for the throne from a strong base.

2) After William won at Hastings, he built castles all over England as he marched around the country establishing his rule.

3) There were lots of different reasons for building so many castles:

> Pevensey Castle was built using timber that was prepared then brought from Normandy. This shows how much planning and preparation went into the invasion.

- Some castles were built to prevent invasion. Castles along the south coast (e.g. Dover, Arundel, Corfe) helped to protect England from an invasion by sea, while castles in the Marcher earldoms (e.g. Chester, Shrewsbury, Hereford) were built to prevent a Welsh invasion (see p.20).
- Castles were often built as a response to Anglo-Saxon rebellions. For example, William built a castle in Exeter after defeating an uprising in the town in 1068.
- Castles were also a highly visible symbol of the Normans' dominance and control over England.

4) More than two-thirds of Norman castles were built in towns — this helped the Normans to control the urban population.

5) Norman castles were sometimes built on the sites of Anglo-Saxon thegns' residences. From a practical perspective, this meant that the Normans could reuse existing fortifications. However, it was also a symbol that they had replaced the Anglo-Saxons as rulers.

6) There are approximately fifty castles recorded in Domesday Book (see p.44), and all but one of them were built between 1066 and 1086. Many more castles and fortifications were built in this period but weren't recorded in Domesday Book.

Most of the Norman castles were motte and bailey castles (see p.24).

Castles were a Key Part of the Normans' Military Strategy

Castles were vital in the early stages of the Norman Conquest — their defensive and military features were very useful when William was struggling to put down Anglo-Saxon resistance and establish himself as king.

1) The Normans used castles as strong defensive positions, which helped them to hold their ground against Anglo-Saxon attacks.

2) They also used castles to control strategically important places (e.g. towns, major roads and rivers) so that Normans across the country couldn't get cut off from each other. This made it very hard for Anglo-Saxon rebels to move around the country freely.

3) The network of castles throughout England meant that William could station Norman troops all over the country. This meant that troops could be sent quickly to deal with local unrest — this happened in the south and west in 1069, when William was busy putting down a revolt in northern England (see p.26).

4) Castles weren't just defensive — they were also used as bases so Norman troops could launch attacks on the surrounding territory. This helped the Normans to bring more land under their control.

> 'The fortifications called castles by the Normans were scarcely known in the English provinces, and so the English — in spite of their courage and love of fighting — could put up only a weak resistance to their enemies.'
> Orderic Vitalis (a 12th-century historian)

Comment and Analysis

The Anglo-Saxons didn't have much experience of warfare involving castles and they didn't have many strong fortifications that they could hold against the Normans. This gave the Normans a big military advantage over the Anglo-Saxons.

William I in Power: Securing the Kingdom, 1066-1087

Norman Castles

SKILLS PRACTICE

The Normans built castles for many purposes — have a go at the activities below to see if you know all of the reasons why castles were built and how they helped the Normans keep control of England.

Knowledge and Understanding

1) Copy and complete the table below, giving as much detail as possible about why the following castles were built.

Castles	Why they were built
a) Pevensey, Hastings	
b) Dover, Arundel, Corfe	
c) Chester, Shrewsbury, Hereford	
d) Exeter	

2) What information does Domesday Book give about Norman castles?

3) Explain why the Normans' use of castles put the Anglo-Saxons at a military disadvantage.

Thinking Historically

1) Explain how each of the following aspects of castles helped the Normans gain and keep control of England.
   a) They were used to control important locations like towns and roads.
   b) There was a large network of castles throughout England.
   c) They were used as bases to launch attacks.

2) How did castles symbolise the strength of the Normans? You can use the factors in the boxes below to help you write your answer.

> Purpose of castles   Where castles were built   Number of castles

EXAM TIP

Maybe William just appreciated a nice castle...

When writing longer answers, introduce each new point by referring back to what the question is asking — this will keep you on track and show the examiner why your points are relevant.

William I in Power: Securing the Kingdom, 1066-1087

The Design of Norman Castles

Norman castles were designed to combine military strength with living accommodation. They had to be easy to defend, but also practical for people to live and work inside them.

Most Norman Castles in England were Motte and Bailey Castles

The motte was a large cone-shaped mound of earth with a flat top. Mottes ranged from about 3m to 30m in height. They were usually manmade, but some used the natural features of the landscape.

A tower (sometimes called a keep) was built on top of the motte.

The bailey was a large enclosure. It was usually located on one side of the motte, but the motte was sometimes built inside the bailey.

Like the motte, the bailey was built on raised earthworks (where earth was built up to create a mound or defensive banking).

High walls were built around the motte and bailey. These were often made from a fence of sharpened wooden stakes (a palisade).

The entrance was guarded by a gatehouse.

The motte and bailey were surrounded by ditches, which were sometimes filled with water to create a moat. Often ditches also separated the motte from the bailey. This meant the motte could still be defended even if the bailey was captured.

The entrance to the castle was via a bridge across the ditch or moat. You could only get to the motte through the bailey.

There wasn't much space on the motte, so most of the living accommodation was within the bailey. This could include housing, stables and a chapel.

© Historic England / Mary Evans

Castles Weren't all the Same

Although the motte and bailey design was very common, Norman castles varied in size, structure, building materials and location.

Size
Some Norman castles were large and complex. However, many others were small and simple — they just had a low motte that was topped with a simple wooden structure.

Structure
Norman castles didn't all use the motte and bailey design. For example, Exeter Castle didn't have a motte or keep — it was just a fortified enclosure.

Building Materials
The earliest Norman castles were almost all built from wood and earth. This meant they could be built quickly and without skilled labour. Lots of wooden castles were replaced with stone castles later on. For example, in 1070, William ordered that Hastings Castle should be rebuilt using stone.

Location
Sometimes, the Normans used natural parts of the landscape to make their castles easier to defend. For example, Richmond Castle was built next to a steep drop into the River Swale. They also reused existing Anglo-Saxon structures. The castles at Pevensey and Exeter were built inside fortifications that had existed before the conquest.

William I in Power: Securing the Kingdom, 1066-1087

The Design of Norman Castles

There are lots of key words and design features related to motte and bailey castles — use these activities to check whether you understand all of the different features of a castle and know what their purpose was.

Knowledge and Understanding

1) Explain what is meant by the following terms:

   a) Motte   b) Bailey   c) Keep

2) Why were the earliest Norman castles built from wood?

3) Not all Norman castles were built in the same way. For each of the following castles, describe one unusual feature of the way it was built.
   a) Richmond
   b) Exeter
   c) Pevensey

Thinking Historically

1) The diagram below shows a plan of how a motte and bailey castle might look if it was viewed from above. Describe each labelled feature and explain why it was important. Give as much detail as possible.

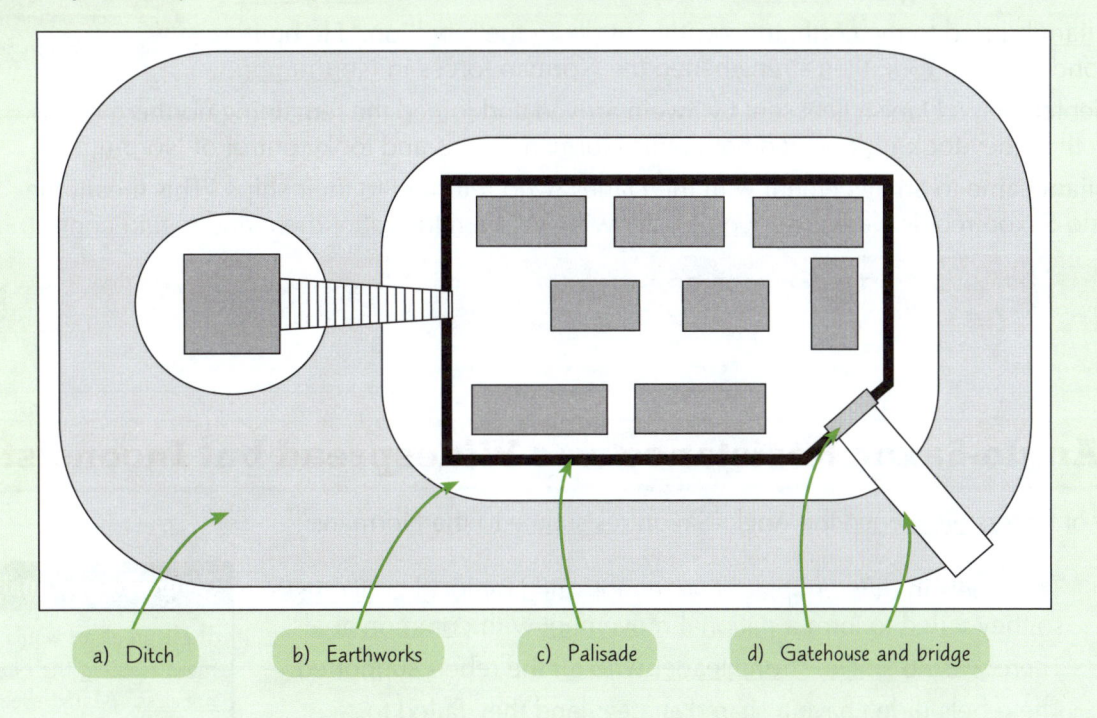

   a) Ditch   b) Earthworks   c) Palisade   d) Gatehouse and bridge

---

EXAM TIP

Make sure you know your motte from your moat...

It's important to be able to describe key features of castles, but you also need to understand the reasons why the Normans built castles and how they helped William to gain control of England.

William I in Power: Securing the Kingdom, 1066-1087

Resistance to Norman Rule, 1068-1069

The Anglo-Saxons were revolting (I know, I can still smell them now...). They wanted their kingdom back after the Normans had seized it. After a few minor rebellions, things suddenly got more serious in 1068.

Edwin and Morcar objected to Norman Rule

1) Edwin of Mercia and Morcar of Northumbria were Anglo-Saxon earls (and brothers) who had submitted to William's rule in 1066 (see p.20). William had kept them close to him in the royal household since then.
2) However, Edwin and Morcar felt frustrated with William for restricting their power. In 1068, they fled the royal household to launch a major rebellion in Mercia, with the support of a Welsh lord named Bleddyn.
3) William responded immediately by marching into Mercia and building a castle in Warwick. This caused Edwin and Morcar to surrender to William once again.
4) William decided to be lenient towards the brothers by granting them their lives and their freedom. He went to Nottingham and York in order to start construction on two more castles, before returning south.

Comment and Analysis

William might have regretted his mild response to this rebellion later on, as Edwin and Morcar started another rebellion in Mercia during the northern revolt in 1069.

There was a Major Revolt in Northern England in 1069

1) In 1069, a group of northern nobles joined forces with Edgar Atheling, King Malcolm III of Scotland and King Swein II of Denmark in a major rebellion, which posed a serious threat to William's rule.
2) Early in 1069, the rebels massacred the newly-appointed Norman Earl of Northumbria and several hundred of his knights at Durham. They then moved south to besiege York.
3) William hurried to the north and swiftly put down the rebellion. He built a second castle at York, then strengthened the Norman forces in Northumbria.

For more on the response to this rebellion, see p.28.

4) In September, a Danish fleet sent by Swein arrived and joined the remaining northern rebels. Together, they took York, seized both of its Norman castles and took control of Northumbria.
5) William came to an agreement with the Danes, who returned to their ships. This meant the Anglo-Saxon rebels were unsupported, allowing William to scatter them and regain control.

There was also unrest in other places — an Anglo-Saxon thegn called Eadric the Wild attacked Shrewsbury, and there were other risings in the west country. William's local forces dealt with the unrest in the south and west, while William marched to the north.

The Anglo-Saxon Resistance was Widespread but Inconsistent

A range of factors weakened the Anglo-Saxon resistance to the Normans:

- The rebels in different places were motivated by local concerns, so they failed to form a national movement with common goals.
- There was no single, strong leader who all the rebels supported.
- The rebels didn't have a shared strategy and they failed to coordinate their uprisings, making it easier to defeat them.
- Many English nobles actually supported William and some even helped him to fight the rebels. Others just didn't take sides at all.

Comment and Analysis

These problems would eventually make resisting the Normans seem hopeless. Many rebels were killed or forced into exile, and those who remained in England may have gradually started to accept that the Normans had come to stay.

William I in Power: Securing the Kingdom, 1066-1087

Resistance to Norman Rule, 1068-1069

SKILLS PRACTICE

There are lots of important names associated with rebellions against the Normans. These activities will make sure you know all of the people who were involved and how they tried to take down William.

Knowledge and Understanding

1) Copy and complete the table below, stating who fought against the Normans in Mercia in 1068 and in Northumbria in 1069.

Mercia, 1068	Northumbria, 1069

2) The flowchart below shows the key events that took place during the northern rebellion in 1069. Copy and complete the flowchart by adding the missing events.

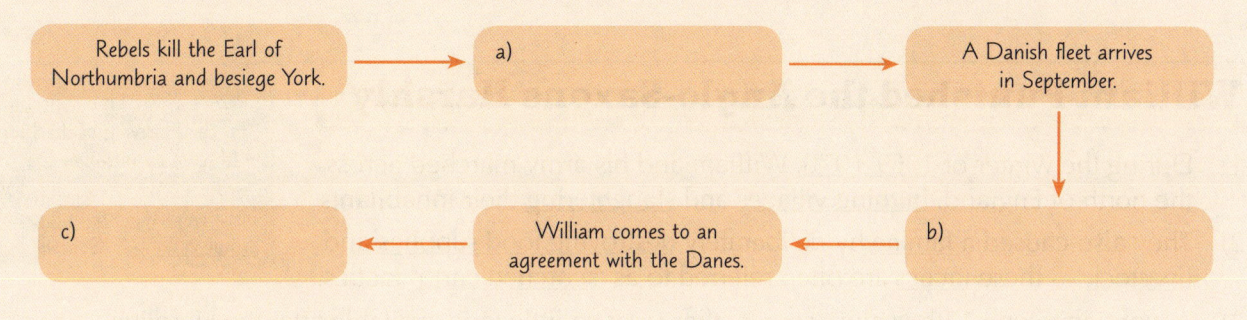

Rebels kill the Earl of Northumbria and besiege York. → a) → A Danish fleet arrives in September. ↓ c) ← William comes to an agreement with the Danes. ← b)

Thinking Historically

1) At first, William tried to work with the Anglo-Saxon nobles (see page 20). How do the actions of Edwin and Morcar show the difficulties that William faced in working with Anglo-Saxon nobles?

2) Explain why the Anglo-Saxon resistance was ineffective.

3) What do you think was the main reason for the failure of the northern revolt in 1069? Explain your answer.

EXAM TIP

William made more enemies after he became king...

When you're writing about why a particular event happened — for example, the rebellion in northern England in 1069 — think about the events that led up to it and why they happened.

William I in Power: Securing the Kingdom, 1066-1087

The Harrying of the North

William's response to the revolt in 1069 was merciless, but effective. It put an end to resistance in the north and cemented his authority as king, just when he was starting to feel the pressure...

The 1069 Revolt led to the Harrying of the North

1) William had tried to keep as many Anglo-Saxon nobles on his side as he could after the conquest (see p.20). However, the northern revolt in 1069 showed that William's approach wasn't working.
2) The northern revolt was an unprecedented threat to William's authority, because the rebels in the north were also supported by powerful foreign forces, including the Scots and the Danes.
3) William was facing other rebellions all over the country at the time. This meant that he needed to act quickly and decisively.
4) These developments forced William to change his approach to the Anglo-Saxons. He decided to lay waste to large parts of the north, so they would be forced to submit to the Normans. This ruthless approach became known as the 'Harrying of the North'.

Comment and Analysis
William's goal was to avoid any future rebellion in the north by destroying the rebels' supplies and sources of support. The Harrying also sent a powerful message to the rest of the country about what to expect if they rebelled.

William Punished the Anglo-Saxons Harshly

1) During the winter of 1069-1070, William and his army marched across the north of England, burning villages and slaughtering their inhabitants.
2) They also caused a famine by deliberately destroying food supplies and livestock — these tactics are often referred to as 'scorched earth' tactics.
3) According to one 12th-century source, there was so little food available after the Harrying of the North that the remaining Anglo-Saxons had to eat dogs, cats and horses to survive.
4) This destruction stretched across a huge area. While the majority of the Harrying took place in Yorkshire and the north east, the damage also reached Lincolnshire, Cheshire and Staffordshire.

People at the time criticised William for the Harrying of the North. The 12th-century historian Orderic Vitalis wrote 'I have often praised William... but I can say nothing good about this brutal slaughter. God will punish him.'

- The Harrying is often seen as evidence of the 'Norman Yoke'. This refers to the idea that the Normans brutally oppressed the Anglo-Saxons using methods that were unnecessarily cruel.
- However, laying waste to enemy territory was a common military tactic in the 11th century. Some historians argue that we shouldn't judge William's actions by modern moral standards.

The Harrying had Short-Term and Long-Term Consequences

1) It's clear from the sources that the Harrying of the North was a brutal campaign which caused suffering for those who were caught up in it.
2) In the short term, many northerners fled from the destruction and became refugees, settling elsewhere in England or the south of Scotland. The people who stayed in the north faced disease and starvation.
3) Some northerners joined other pockets of resistance such as Hereward the Wake's East Anglian rebellion (see p.30), but the resistance didn't last for long.
4) In 1086, many northern villages were described as 'waste' in Domesday Book (see p.44). Some historians use this to argue that the Harrying caused long-term damage to the northern economy, because Domesday Book was made almost twenty years later.

Comment and Analysis
There were lots of reasons why a village might have been described as 'waste' in Domesday Book (e.g. if it didn't pay taxes), so it's difficult to assess whether the Harrying caused any serious long-term damage.

William I in Power: Securing the Kingdom, 1066-1087

The Harrying of the North

Use the activities on this page to really nail down what you've learnt about the Harrying of the North.

Knowledge and Understanding

1) In your own words, explain what the Harrying of the North was.

2) Using the key words below, explain why William carried out the Harrying of the North.

   deter   threat   rebellions   supplies

Thinking Historically

1) How did William's reaction to the 1069 revolt differ from his reaction to previous rebellions?

2) Copy and complete the mind map below, listing the consequences of the Harrying of the North.

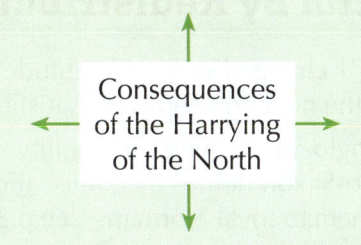

   ← Consequences of the Harrying of the North →

3) Copy and complete the table below, giving evidence for and against each statement about the Harrying of the North.

Statement	Evidence for	Evidence against
a) The Harrying of the North is evidence of the 'Norman Yoke'.		
b) Domesday Book is a helpful source for analysing the damage caused by the Harrying.		

4) Do you think William could have maintained control of England without the Harrying of the North? Explain your answer. You can use other pages in this section to help you.

The Anglo-Saxons had got on William's last nerve...

Making essay plans can be a useful way of revising — if you can't think of much to write when you're planning an essay answer, it might mean that you need a quick recap of the topic.

William I in Power: Securing the Kingdom, 1066-1087

Resistance to Norman Rule, 1070-1071

Anglo-Saxon resistance was starting to wind down by 1070, but Hereward the Wake had other ideas...

Hereward the Wake led an East Anglian Rebellion

1) In 1070, there was an uprising in East Anglia led by an Anglo-Saxon thegn known as Hereward the Wake, whose lands had been confiscated after the Norman Conquest.

2) Hereward was supported by the Danes, who had arrived in East Anglia in 1070. However, William paid the Danes to make them abandon Hereward.

3) In 1071, Hereward was joined by more Anglo-Saxon rebels, including Morcar (see p.26). They went to the Isle of Ely and tried to hold it against William's army.

4) William's forces besieged the island and defeated the rebels. Morcar was captured and imprisoned.

5) Hereward survived the attack on Ely, but not much is known about his fate afterwards. However, he doesn't seem to have taken part in any further resistance. Hereward's uprising was the last major rebellion to happen until 1075 (see p.32).

Some sources on Hereward the Wake say that he surrendered to William, who pardoned him.

William maintained control by Redistributing Land...

1) The rebellions between 1068 and 1071 changed William's attitude to the Anglo-Saxons. He no longer felt the need to keep them satisfied.

2) William stopped trying to integrate Anglo-Saxons into the nobility — instead, he started replacing the Anglo-Saxon nobles by confiscating (taking away) their lands and giving them to loyal Normans (see p.38).

The redistribution of land is one example of a process known as Normanisation — William made England 'more Norman' by replacing Anglo-Saxons with Normans in areas such as government and the Church.

Comment and Analysis
These changes to landownership were particularly important in places that were vulnerable to invasion or serious unrest, such as the Marcher earldoms (see p.20).

3) At the same time, William changed the size and shape of English estates. In Anglo-Saxon England, some lords had held vast areas of land, whereas others had held lands that were scattered across several shires. William reorganised these large areas of land into much smaller estates that were limited to a single region.

4) He also increased the proportion of English land held by the king and limited the amount of land that each noble family could hold.

5) These changes helped William to maintain control because compact estates were much easier to defend. Giving noble families smaller areas of land also strengthened William's own position — by restricting the power of these families, he ensured that none of them were strong enough to threaten his position as king.

...and by strengthening his position in Government

1) William made his hold on the kingdom more secure through centralisation. This increased William's personal control of the government.

The way William ruled Norman England is covered in more detail on pages 36-40.

2) William didn't change much about the Anglo-Saxon system of government. However, he did replace all of the Anglo-Saxons in government with Normans who were loyal to him.

3) He also used castles (see p.22-24) to govern the kingdom more effectively. The lords in charge of castles were made responsible for governing the surrounding area. As a result, many castles were centres of local government, where taxes were collected and law and order was enforced.

4) Having established his authority in England, William felt comfortable going back to Normandy. He used regents (see p.38) to govern the kingdom during these absences, which became more and more frequent.

William I in Power: Securing the Kingdom, 1066-1087

Resistance to Norman Rule, 1070-1071

SKILLS PRACTICE

Test your knowledge of Normanisation and the reaction to the Anglo-Saxon rebellions with these activities.

Knowledge and Understanding

1) Copy and complete the flowchart below, adding the missing information about the rebellion led by Hereward the Wake.

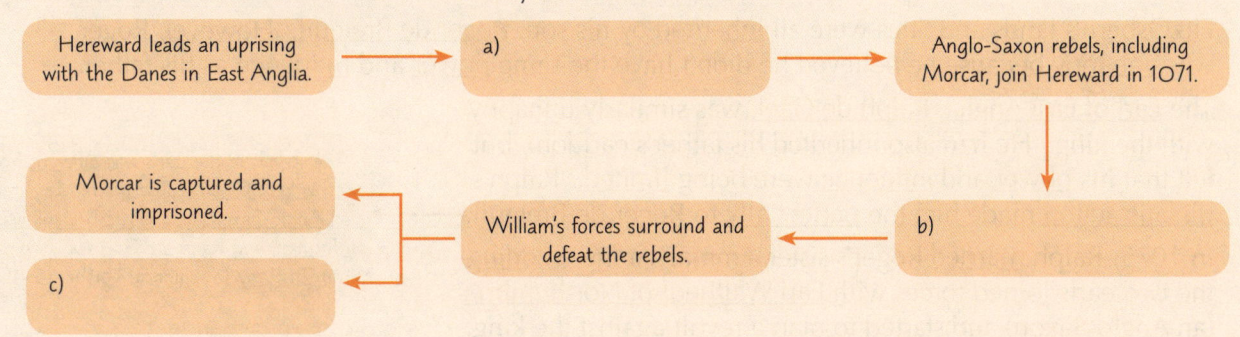

   - Hereward leads an uprising with the Danes in East Anglia. → a) → Anglo-Saxon rebels, including Morcar, join Hereward in 1071.
   - Morcar is captured and imprisoned. ← William's forces surround and defeat the rebels. ← b)
   - c)

2) How did William's attitude towards the Anglo-Saxons change as a result of the rebellions between 1068 and 1071?

3) Explain what is meant by the term 'Normanisation'.

4) Copy and complete the mind map below, adding the ways that William redistributed land.

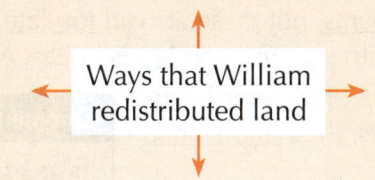

   Ways that William redistributed land

Thinking Historically

1) Explain how William's redistribution of land helped him to maintain control over England. Give as much detail as possible.

2) Copy and complete the table below, explaining how each of the following aspects of government helped to strengthen William's control.

Aspect of government	How this strengthened William's control
a) Centralisation	
b) Normanisation	
c) Use of castles	

William took control through centralisation...

Make sure you don't mix up the details of the different rebellions. For example, the revolt in northern England was in 1069, whereas Hereward the Wake rebelled in East Anglia in 1070.

William I in Power: Securing the Kingdom, 1066-1087

The Revolt of the Earls

Just when William thought he'd dealt with all the unrest, some of his own nobles decided to join the party...

Some of William's Earls started to Resent Him

1) In 1071, William FitzOsbern (one of the king's closest allies) died. FitzOsbern was the Earl of Hereford, but he also held other lands in the south and west of the country. This made him a very powerful figure.
2) FitzOsbern's lands and titles were all inherited by his son, Roger de Breteuil. However, Roger was unhappy because he believed he didn't have the same power and influence as his father.
3) The Earl of East Anglia, Ralph de Gael, was similarly unhappy with the king. He had also inherited his father's earldom, but felt that his power and influence were being limited. Ralph's dissatisfaction made him the perfect ally to Roger de Breteuil.
4) In 1075, Ralph married Roger's sister, Emma. At the wedding, the two earls joined forces with Earl Waltheof of Northumbria (an Anglo-Saxon) and started to plan a revolt against the king.

> The Revolt of the Earls was different from other rebellions because the rebels weren't all Anglo-Saxons. Roger de Breteuil was a Norman, and Ralph de Gael was originally from Brittany (a region in northern France).

The Revolt went Wrong from the Start

1) Waltheof's involvement in the revolt was short-lived. He travelled to Normandy to meet King William and confessed the plan to him.
2) William gave the information to Archbishop Lanfranc, who was acting as regent (see p.38) in England. This allowed Lanfranc to react quickly, trapping Roger and Ralph in their earldoms.
3) Ralph was under siege in Norwich Castle, but he escaped and left his wife (Emma) in control. He went to Denmark for reinforcements, but these arrived too late. After a long siege, Emma surrendered. She and Ralph agreed to give up their lands in East Anglia, then went into exile.
4) Meanwhile, Roger barely made it out of Hereford. He was captured by William's supporters, then imprisoned for life for his disloyalty to the king.
5) Despite confessing, Waltheof was beheaded for taking part in the revolt. He became the only member of the Anglo-Saxon nobility to be executed in William's reign.

> **Comment and Analysis**
> It's uncertain why Waltheof was punished more harshly than Roger and Ralph. Anglo-Saxons (e.g. Edwin and Morcar, see p.26) had rebelled against the king in the past, but William treated them more leniently.

The Revolt of the Earls could have been a Serious Threat

1) The Revolt of the Earls had the potential to be a serious threat to William's rule. The earls involved held extensive lands across the kingdom, and they had Anglo-Saxon, Norman and Danish support.
2) However, this threat never became a reality. The revolt failed for several reasons:

- Anglo-Saxon support for the revolt wasn't widespread enough — not many Anglo-Saxons were willing to put themselves at risk to increase the power and influence of foreign earls.
- Earl Waltheof of Northumbria betrayed Roger and Ralph by confessing the plan to William.
- William and Lanfranc's response to the revolt was quick and effective. Roger and Ralph didn't make it out of their earldoms with their armies.
- The Danes arrived in England too late to provide support to the rebels.

3) William was in Normandy when the Revolt of the Earls happened, but it was so easily defeated that he didn't even return to England.
4) The Revolt of the Earls was the last major rebellion to involve Anglo-Saxons in William's reign. After Waltheof's execution, they may have realised they had no choice but to cooperate with the Normans.

William I in Power: Securing the Kingdom, 1066-1087

The Revolt of the Earls

The Revolt of the Earls was the last major challenge against William during his reign as king. Use these activities to test what you know about the different people involved and why the revolt wasn't a success.

Knowledge and Understanding

1) Why did Roger de Breteuil and Ralph de Gael decide to revolt?

2) Make a flashcard for each person below. Write their name on one side and describe their role in the Revolt of the Earls on the other.

   a) Roger de Breteuil
   b) Ralph de Gael
   c) Emma de Gael
   d) Earl Waltheof
   e) Archbishop Lanfranc
   f) The Danes

3) Where was William during the Revolt of the Earls?

4) Explain how Waltheof's punishment was different from Roger de Breteuil's and Ralph de Gael's.

Thinking Historically

1) Why do you think the Revolt of the Earls was the last major rebellion against William to involve the Anglo-Saxons?

2) Copy and complete the table below, listing reasons why the northern revolt in 1069 (see page 26) and the Revolt of the Earls in 1075 posed a threat to William's rule.

Northern Revolt, 1069	The Revolt of the Earls, 1075

3) Do you think the northern revolt in 1069 or the Revolt of the Earls in 1075 was a bigger threat to William's rule? Explain your answer.

EXAM TIP

William was disgusted by the revolting Earls...

In the British Depth Study section of your exam, part c) will have two questions to choose from. You only need to answer one of these — you won't get extra marks for answering both of them.

William I in Power: Securing the Kingdom, 1066-1087

Worked Exam-Style Question

This worked answer will help you answer the 4-mark question. Remember that you need to identify two separate features of the topic mentioned in the question and give some extra information about each feature.

Describe two aspects of the Harrying of the North. [4 marks]

Identify an aspect, then add some supporting information that gives a bit more detail.

One aspect of the Harrying of the North was the Normans' use of 'scorched earth' tactics. These tactics were used to destroy food supplies and livestock, causing a famine in northern England.

Another aspect of the Harrying of the North was that the Normans burned villages across a large area of Yorkshire and the north east. Many of the northerners who lost their homes became refugees and fled to other parts of England or to the south of Scotland.

Make sure the supporting information is closely related to the aspect you have identified.

William I in Power: Securing the Kingdom, 1066-1087

Exam-Style Questions

Try these exam-style questions to practise everything you've learned about how William secured power in England. For questions 2 and 3, remember to write about factors not mentioned in the prompt points.

Exam-Style Questions

1) Describe two aspects of the Marcher earldoms.   [4 marks]

2) Explain why the Revolt of the Earls in 1075 failed.

   You could mention:
   - Anglo-Saxon support
   - Earl Waltheof

   You should also use your own knowledge.   [12 marks]

3) 'The main reason William I stayed in power was the failure of the Anglo-Saxons to form a national movement against him.'

   To what extent do you agree with this statement? Explain your answer.

   You could mention:
   - castles
   - Normanisation

   You should also use your own knowledge.   [16 marks]

Norman England, 1066-1088

Norman Society

William established his rule through a mixture of change and continuity from the Anglo-Saxon system.

William Changed the Social Structure of England

1) After 1066, William kept the Anglo-Saxon idea of giving out land in exchange for service. However, he changed the structure of the existing system (see p.4) so the king had overall control and ownership of all the land, which he could give out or take away as he chose.

2) Historians often refer to the new social structure as the feudal system. There was a clear hierarchy, like in Anglo-Saxon England, but some of the roles changed slightly.

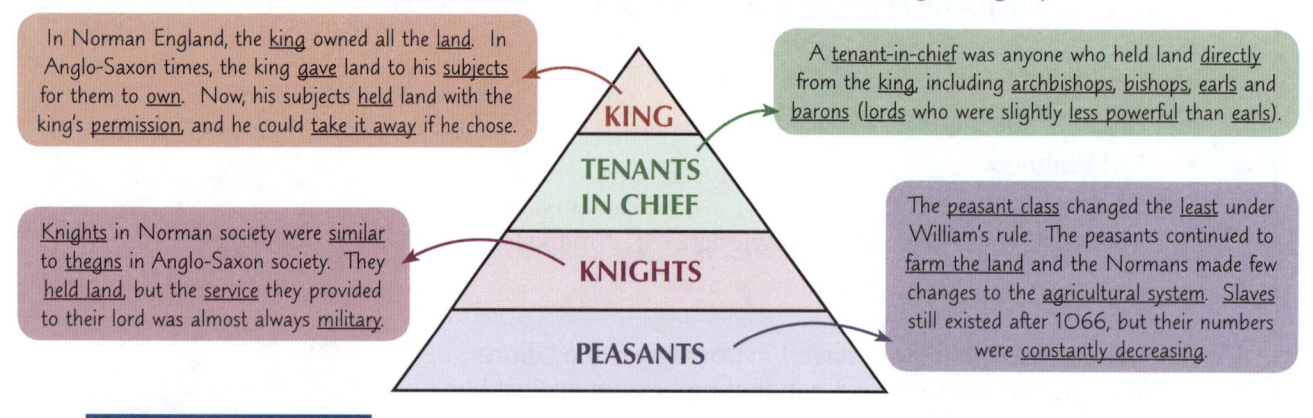

In Norman England, the king owned all the land. In Anglo-Saxon times, the king gave land to his subjects for them to own. Now, his subjects held land with the king's permission, and he could take it away if he chose.

KING
TENANTS IN CHIEF
KNIGHTS
PEASANTS

A tenant-in-chief was anyone who held land directly from the king, including archbishops, bishops, earls and barons (lords who were slightly less powerful than earls).

Knights in Norman society were similar to thegns in Anglo-Saxon society. They held land, but the service they provided to their lord was almost always military.

The peasant class changed the least under William's rule. The peasants continued to farm the land and the Normans made few changes to the agricultural system. Slaves still existed after 1066, but their numbers were constantly decreasing.

Comment and Analysis

These changes to the social structure of England were intended to create a large network of loyal supporters who could provide military service to the king. This was crucially important in helping William to secure the conquest.

The Feudal System was designed to Reward Loyal Service

1) The feudal system was based on vassalic bonds. The king and his lords gave land to their subjects (vassals) in return for their loyalty.

2) Tenants-in-chief were the king's vassals. They did homage to the king by kneeling before him and swearing loyalty to him. They also provided knights when the king needed them and shared a portion of the income from their land with him.

3) Knights were the tenants-in-chief's vassals. In return for land, knights had to do homage and pay taxes, as well as providing military service to their lord. This service might involve protecting a castle, fighting in wars or keeping their lord safe while travelling.

4) Most peasants worked for a lord by providing labour service on his land. In return, they were given their lord's protection and the right to farm a small patch of land for themselves. However, they still had to pay taxes and give their lord a share of the crops. Although peasants didn't formally do homage to their lord, they were still expected to be loyal.

A vassal was someone who swore an oath of loyalty to their lord during a ceremony called homage. In return, the lord swore an oath to protect the vassal.

The Normans encouraged loyalty within the feudal system by using forfeiture — if a vassal broke the agreement between them and their lord, they might be forced to forfeit (give up) their land. William had been using forfeiture since 1066 in order to remove Anglo-Saxons who opposed him, but he was fully prepared to punish disloyal Normans in the same way.

Norman Society

Loyalty was an important feature of William's feudal system. Try these activities to make sure you know the Norman hierarchy in detail and how it compared to the Anglo-Saxon social structure that came before it.

Knowledge and Understanding

The diagram below shows the social hierarchy in Norman England.

1) Copy and complete the diagram, stating what sort of people were at each level in the hierarchy and adding as much extra information about the people at this level as you can.

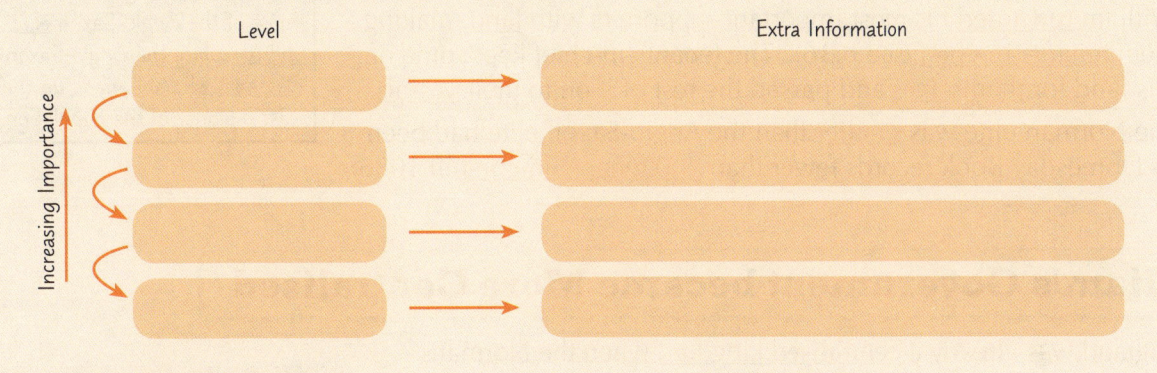

Level → Extra Information (Increasing Importance)

2) Using the key words below, explain how the feudal system encouraged loyalty.

vassals   homage   forfeiture

Thinking Historically

1) Copy and complete the table below, explaining whether there was change or continuity in each aspect of society between Anglo-Saxon England (see p.4) and Norman England.

Aspect of society	Change or continuity?	Explanation for choice
a) Ownership of land		
b) Role of a lord		
c) Work done by peasants		
d) Number of slaves		

2) Why did the king in Norman society have more power than the king in Anglo-Saxon society? Explain your answer.

EXAM TIP

The royalty demanded loyalty...

It's good to know how things changed or stayed the same, but you should also learn why this was the case — e.g. William changed how society was structured to give himself more control.

Norman England, 1066-1088

Norman Government

Once the conquest was complete, William had to decide how to govern the country he'd taken over.

The Anglo-Saxon Elite was Replaced with Normans

1) After 1066, William tried to work with the Anglo-Saxon elite, but he gave up on this policy after a series of major rebellions (see p.26-30).
2) Around 1070, William started to systematically replace Anglo-Saxon nobles with Normans. Domesday Book (see p.44) shows that almost all the Anglo-Saxon elite had been replaced with Normans by 1086.
3) William rewarded his most important supporters with land, making them tenants-in-chief (see p.36). The tenants-in-chief kept some of this land for themselves and passed the rest of it on to their vassals.
4) The Norman elite was smaller than the Anglo-Saxon elite had been — Domesday Book records fewer than 200 tenants-in-chief in 1086.

Comment and Analysis

The Normans only ever made up a small minority of the population of England. Although they forced out most of the Anglo-Saxon elite, they didn't replace the Anglo-Saxon peasants who still made up the vast majority of the population.

William's Government became More Centralised

1) England was already a centralised kingdom when the Normans invaded. William kept the structure of the existing government, but filled it with Normans rather than Anglo-Saxons. William also used certain features of Anglo-Saxon government more effectively.

Centralisation is when power becomes focused around one figure — in this case, the king.

2) For example, William increased the use of writs (short documents containing royal commands for local government officials to follow). These were common in Anglo-Saxon England, but hadn't been used in Normandy. The use of writs allowed William to take a more direct role in running the whole kingdom.
3) William also kept England divided into shires and hundreds, but increased the power of the sheriffs who were responsible for running them (see p.40).

William had a small 'inner circle' of loyal supporters who held around a quarter of England, but even these lands weren't as big as the earldoms (e.g. Northumbria and Mercia) that had existed in Anglo-Saxon England.

4) By giving more power to the sheriffs, William limited the power of the earls. There were fewer earls in Norman England than there had been in Anglo-Saxon England, and they held smaller earldoms. The sheriffs started to take over some of their responsibilities in local government.
5) These changes gave William more control, as they provided him with strong, loyal supporters all over England to enforce his rule. However, they stopped anyone from becoming strong enough to challenge him.

William used Regents to rule in his Absence

1) William was King of England, but he was also Duke of Normandy. This meant he needed to divide his time between these territories.
2) William needed someone to govern England while he was away, which is why he used regents — a regent is someone who rules on the king's behalf, with the same authority as the king himself.
3) As a result, the regents had to be trusted. For example, William appointed close supporters like his half-brother Odo of Bayeux (see p.50) and Archbishop Lanfranc of Canterbury (see p.48) as regents whenever he left the kingdom for a long period of time.

It's difficult to tell exactly how much time William spent in England, but most historians suggest that he spent the majority of his reign away from the kingdom. This makes the role of William's regents particularly important in the government of Norman England.

One of the reasons William went to Normandy so often was to fight against rivals in northern France.

Norman England, 1066-1088

Norman Government

SKILLS PRACTICE

Once in charge, William made many changes to ensure he could control England effectively — the activities below will help you understand the different things William did to run his government.

Knowledge and Understanding

1) Give one similarity between the population of Anglo-Saxon England and the population of Norman England.

2) Explain what is meant by a centralised government.

3) Explain how the lands held by William's 'inner circle' of loyal supporters compared to the lands held by earls in Anglo-Saxon England.

4) Using the key words and phrases below, explain how William used regents to govern England.

   Normandy   same authority   Odo of Bayeux   Archbishop Lanfranc

Thinking Historically

1) Why do you think the Anglo-Saxon rebellions (see pages 26-30) encouraged William to replace Anglo-Saxon nobles with Norman nobles?

2) Copy and complete the mind map below, giving as much detail as possible about how William changed each aspect of government to increase his power.

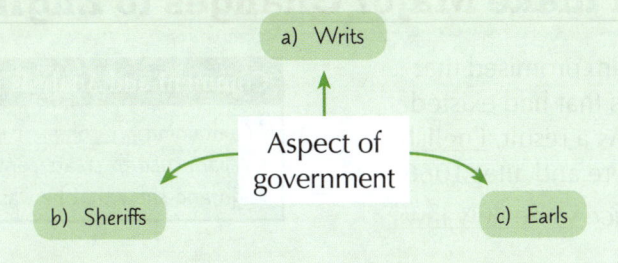

   a) Writs
   b) Sheriffs
   c) Earls

   (Aspect of government)

EXAM TIP

There was a new elite in town...
When you're writing in the exam, only use the most relevant examples to back up your points. There should be a clear link between the examples you use and the point you're making.

Norman England, 1066-1088

Norman Government

William kept several aspects of Anglo-Saxon government after the Norman Conquest, but changed the roles of the people who were responsible for putting the system into practice.

Sheriffs had an Increased Role in Local Government

1) The role of sheriff already existed in Anglo-Saxon England (see p.4), and it didn't change a lot under the Normans — they helped to govern at a local level. Their role included:

- Supervising the collection of fines and taxes
- Judging civil or criminal cases in local courts
- Organising (and often leading) military forces

> **Comment and Analysis**
>
> Giving more power to sheriffs meant that earls had less influence over how their lands were managed. This led to resentment — some historians believe it was one of the main reasons for the Revolt of the Earls in 1075 (see p.32).

2) Under the Normans, sheriffs were able to perform their duties with less interference from the earls. This was because William had reduced the power of the earls to give himself complete authority as king (see p.38).

3) As in Anglo-Saxon England, sheriffs were directly appointed by the king. However, William usually appointed people who were wealthier and held more land than Anglo-Saxon sheriffs.

4) William had to be careful about giving the sheriffs too much power. They needed enough authority to perform their duties, but they might be able to rebel against the king if they became too powerful.

Sheriffs were Responsible for the Royal Demesne

1) When William took ownership of all the land in England (see p.36), he kept around one quarter of it for himself. This land was called the royal demesne.

2) One new responsibility for William's sheriffs was to manage the royal demesne, which was typically worked by poorer peasants.

3) Some sheriffs were given extra lands or even castles when they were appointed, granting them wealth and power as well as status. However, some of them took advantage of their role, using it to take even more land or money for themselves.

> The word 'demesne' refers to any land that a lord kept for his own personal use, rather than giving it to a vassal.

The Normans Didn't make Major Changes to English Law

1) When he became king, William promised that he would not change the laws that had existed during King Edward's reign. As a result, English law was almost the same before and after 1066.

> **Comment and Analysis**
>
> Maintaining pre-conquest law was another way that William tried to create continuity with King Edward's reign and show that he was Edward's legitimate successor.

2) However, William did introduce some new laws:

- He introduced forest law, which set aside large areas of the country as 'royal forest' for the king to hunt in.
- The royal forest wasn't just woodland — it included any land that was set aside as hunting grounds. Ordinary people weren't allowed to use the royal forest, and they faced severe punishment for breaking the law.
- William also introduced the 'murdrum' fine to protect Norman settlers from violence. If a Norman was murdered and the killer wasn't caught, then the whole village where he was murdered had to pay a large fine.

> The introduction of forest law was extremely unpopular with ordinary people, as it limited the amount of land available for hunting or gathering food. The Normans even destroyed villages to make land more suitable for hunting, forcing people to leave their homes.

Norman England, 1066-1088

Norman Government

William's changes were great for sheriffs, but not everyone did so well out of these developments. Give these activities a go to make sure you know who benefited from the changes to local government.

Knowledge and Understanding

1) Why did William need to limit how much power he gave to sheriffs?

2) In your own words, explain what the royal demesne was.

3) Explain why William didn't make many changes to Anglo-Saxon laws.

4) Explain the changes below that William made to Anglo-Saxon law.

   a) Forest law   b) Murdrum fine

5) Why was forest law so unpopular with ordinary people?

Thinking Historically

1) Copy and complete the table below, giving ways that sheriffs changed and ways that they stayed the same from Anglo-Saxon England to Norman England.

Change	Continuity

2) 'William's changes to the power of sheriffs helped him maintain control over earls.'

   You can use page 38 to help you.

   a) Write a paragraph agreeing with the statement above.
   b) Write a paragraph disagreeing with the statement above.
   c) Write a conclusion summarising how far you agree with the statement above.

The Normans fined Anglo-Saxons for trying to murdrum...
William was arguably a very successful ruler, but some of his decisions were unpopular — it's important to know how the changes he made as King of England impacted his reign.

Norman England, 1066-1088

Life in Norman England

The Normans brought some major changes to England, but for a lot of people it was just business as usual.

Villages were Hardly Affected by the conquest...

1) For many people, life was very similar to how it had been before the Norman Conquest — the traditional Anglo-Saxon villages were mostly unchanged. The peasants who lived in them still endured harsh living conditions, and their work still revolved around farming their lord's land.

2) However, there were some changes at this level of society. For example, the Normans helped to get rid of slavery — it was already declining in England before 1066, but the Normans accelerated the process. Domesday Book (see p.44) shows that fewer people were slaves in England in 1086 than in 1066.

> **Comment and Analysis**
> Anglo-Saxon experiences of the conquest varied hugely depending on each individual's personal circumstances, including their social status, their gender and where in the country they lived. For example, the experience of a leading member of the Anglo-Saxon elite would have been different from that of one of his peasant farmers.

...but Towns became Increasingly Important

1) Many towns were badly affected by the conquest and the rebellions that followed — buildings were destroyed and the local economy was damaged. In some towns (e.g. York and Lincoln), buildings were torn down to make way for building castles.

2) However, the towns began to recover in the years following the Norman Conquest:

- Many existing towns grew in size (e.g. Nottingham) and multiple new towns developed (e.g. St Albans).
- The larger and wealthier towns (e.g. Canterbury) attracted immigrants from abroad, including merchants and traders. This increase in population and business helped the towns to recover.
- Towns played a more important role in society and the economy than in Anglo-Saxon England — they were centres of trade and administration that also had military and religious functions.

Although more people started living in towns after 1066, most people still lived in villages.

3) Although building castles often meant destroying other buildings, these castles also contributed to the growth of towns. There were soldiers living in them, which helped the economy by creating demand for goods and services. When a castle was built, a new town often developed around it (e.g. Windsor).

There was a lot of Economic Growth

1) As many towns got bigger, markets grew or new markets were established. Some markets were set up in castles, because they provided a secure place to trade. Markets and towns were seen as a sign of a civilised country in the 11th century and their growth signalled a strong economy.

2) The conquest caused an increase in trade with Normandy and the rest of France. England exported products such as wool to other countries and imported goods from abroad such as wine and textiles.

3) The Normans built large numbers of churches and cathedrals (see p.46) — this provided a lot of work for craftsmen and helped the economy to grow.

4) However, not everywhere in England benefited from this economic growth. The conquest created an economic divide between the north and the south of the country. The south had been slightly richer than the north before the invasion in 1066, but by 1086 the gap in wealth had widened significantly.

Many places struggled to recover from the Harrying of the North — see p.28.

Norman England, 1066-1088

Life in Norman England

Villages and towns were affected differently after the Normans conquered England. The activities on the page below will help you understand how economic change came about under the Normans.

Knowledge and Understanding

1) Copy and complete the mind map below, explaining how each factor encouraged economic growth in Norman England.

- Economic growth in Norman England
  - a) Castles
  - b) Churches
  - c) Trade

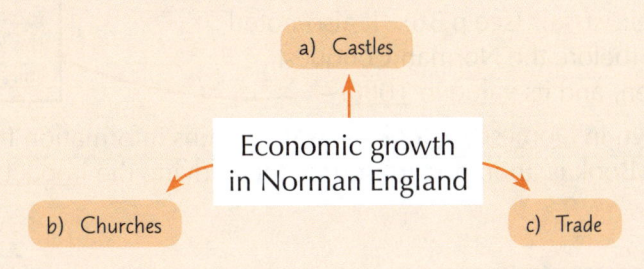

Thinking Historically

1) Explain three ways that towns changed between Anglo-Saxon England and Norman England. Give as much detail as possible.

2) Copy and complete the table below by listing evidence for and against each statement about life in Norman England.

Statement	Evidence for	Evidence against
a) The conquest didn't affect people at the lowest levels of society.		
b) The conquest had a positive impact on England's economy.		
c) Castles were beneficial for English towns.		

3) Explain how far you agree with each statement in the table above, using the evidence in the table to help you.

EXAM TIP

Towns contributed a good deal to economic growth...

In the exam, you only have a limited amount of time to answer each question. If you're spending too long on one question, write a conclusion then move on to the next question.

Norman England, 1066-1088

Domesday Book

Domesday Book (not 'the Domesday Book' — weird, I know) is a detailed survey and valuation of England's land and resources. No other public record on a similar scale was created in England until the 19th century.

Domesday Book records Who owned What

1) In December 1085, William ordered a survey of all the land in England, which was carried out in 1086. This was called the Domesday Survey.
2) The survey recorded the amount of land held by the king, his tenants-in-chief and their vassals (see p.36). It also noted who held the land in 1066 (before the Norman Conquest), how much it was worth then, and its value in 1086.
3) The survey was written down in Domesday Book — as it contains information from both before and after 1066, Domesday Book is an important source for studying the impact of the conquest.

Comment and Analysis

The Domesday Survey was only possible thanks to Anglo-Saxon taxation records and systems of government, such as the way the kingdom was divided into shires and hundreds (see p.4).

Domesday Book took a lot of Organisation

1) To carry out the survey, the tenants-in-chief and government officials in each shire made lists of who owned the land, and commissioners were appointed to compare these lists with existing records.
2) Juries taken from each hundred were called to special meetings of the shire courts, where the commissioners asked them about the ownership and value of the land.
3) These juries were made up of equal numbers of Anglo-Saxons and Normans. This allowed the commissioners to gather accurate information from both before and after the conquest.
4) This information was then compiled into Great Domesday Book (usually just called Domesday Book).

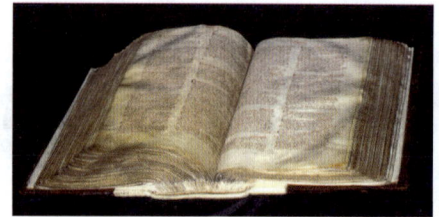

The information helped to Govern the Kingdom

Domesday Book provided the king with financial, legal and military information:

Financial
- Domesday Book allowed the king to make sure that he was receiving all the taxes and other payments that his subjects owed him.
- By creating a detailed record of who owned what and how much their lands were worth, the king could decide whether or not to demand more taxes from certain estates.
- It also helped the king to figure out when someone had inherited land, which allowed him to demand an additional tax from them.

Legal
- Between 1066 and 1086, there had been constant disagreement between Normans and Anglo-Saxons about landownership.
- By creating a detailed record of who owned what, the king could end the disagreements and legalise Norman ownership of the land.
- The survey helped to solve future grievances by providing written evidence of who all the land actually belonged to, rather than having to depend on people's word.

Military
- In 1085, England was facing the threat of an attack by the King of Denmark and his Norwegian allies.
- In order to defend the country, the king needed to know what military resources were available to him. The survey provided vital information, like how many knights the king could summon to fight for him.

Norman England, 1066-1088

Domesday Book

Domesday Book was a useful resource for ruling England — test your knowledge of it with these activities.

Knowledge and Understanding

1) In your own words, explain what Domesday Book is.

2) Explain how the Anglo-Saxon system of government made it possible for the Normans to create Domesday Book.

3) Why is Domesday Book helpful for historians studying the Norman Conquest? Explain your answer.

4) Describe the role each of the following people played in the creation of Domesday Book. Give as much detail as possible.

   a) Tenants-in-chief   b) Commissioners   c) Juries

Thinking Historically

1) Copy and complete the diagram below, explaining how Domesday Book provided a solution to each problem. Give as much detail as you can.

   Problem → **Solution**

   a) The king doesn't know whether he is receiving the correct amount of tax.

   b) An Anglo-Saxon lord and a Norman earl disagree over who owns some land.

   c) The king doesn't know what military resources are available to him.

EXAM TIP

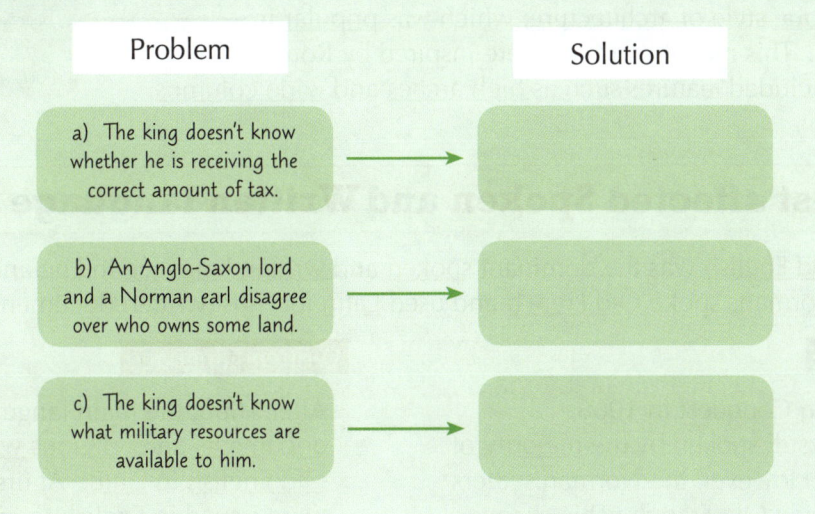

Domesday Book — not as scary as it sounds...

It's important that you know about Domesday Book and feel confident writing about it — make sure you can describe its features and explain why it was important to the Normans.

Norman England, 1066-1088

Norman Culture

The Normans brought more than just soldiers and horses to England — they brought their own culture too...

The Norman Nobility brought Cultural Change

1) The Norman nobility had their own culture and customs, which they brought to England in 1066.
2) This led to changes in areas like food, clothing and even hairstyles. For example, Norman men usually shaved their faces and cut their hair short, whereas Anglo-Saxon men had full beards and long hair.
3) The Normans also brought some new customs to England, such as trial by combat. If someone was accused of a crime, they could challenge their accuser to a fight to the death rather than being judged in a court — the Normans believed that if someone was innocent, then God would intervene and help them to win the fight.

> The nobility (or aristocracy) are the people who belong to the ruling class in society — cultural change wouldn't really have affected those lower in the social hierarchy, like peasants (see p.36).

> **Comment and Analysis**
> Anglo-Saxon culture was considered to be inferior to Norman culture, so the Normans tried to set themselves apart from it as much as they could.

The Church was important in Norman Culture

1) Like in Anglo-Saxon England (see p.6), the Church in Norman England had an important relationship with the nobility. The Normans thought that supporting the Church was a way of serving God.
2) The Norman nobility were generous towards the Church, giving it gifts of land to build on. They also started a church-building programme — within fifty years of the invasion, they had started rebuilding almost all major churches in England, and many parish churches were rebuilt too.
3) The Norman nobility also constructed new monasteries like Shrewsbury Abbey, which was founded in 1083 by the Norman Earl of Shrewsbury, Roger of Montgomery.
4) The Normans built these churches, cathedrals and monasteries in the Romanesque style of architecture, which was popular in Western Europe. This meant that they were inspired by Roman buildings and included features such as high arches and wide columns.

> Durham Cathedral is an example of a church that was rebuilt in the Romanesque style. This style had been introduced to England under King Edward, but it became much more widespread after the conquest.

The Conquest affected Spoken and Written language Differently

1) Before 1066, Old English was the dominant spoken and written language in England. However, the Normans spoke Old French and used Latin for most written documents.

Spoken Language
After the Norman Conquest in 1066, Old English was still spoken by the majority of the population. However, the Norman settlers continued speaking Old French. This changed Old English significantly, because the Normans introduced a large number of French loanwords (words that are brought from one language into another) into English.

Written Language
After 1066, the main language for government documents and religious writing changed from Old English to Latin. At first, royal documents were issued in English to make sure they were understood. William then started to introduce Latin alongside English in bilingual documents. After 1070, these government documents were issued almost exclusively in Latin.

2) These changes to language reflected the Normans' control over England. Within a few years of the conquest, they had completely replaced English in government and in the Church, as well as having a significant impact on the spoken language.

Norman England, 1066-1088

Norman Culture

The Normans affected the culture of England in a number of ways. To help you think about how culture was affected and how significant these changes were, have a go at the activities on this page.

Knowledge and Understanding

1) In your own words, describe what trial by combat was. Give as much detail as possible.

2) Explain how the Normans changed English architecture.

3) Why did the Normans support the Church?

4) Copy and complete the mind map below by adding the different ways that the Normans supported the Church.

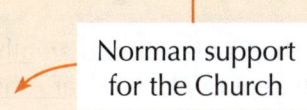

Norman support for the Church

Thinking Historically

1) Copy and complete the diagram below. State how spoken and written language changed after the Norman Conquest and explain why each type of language changed.

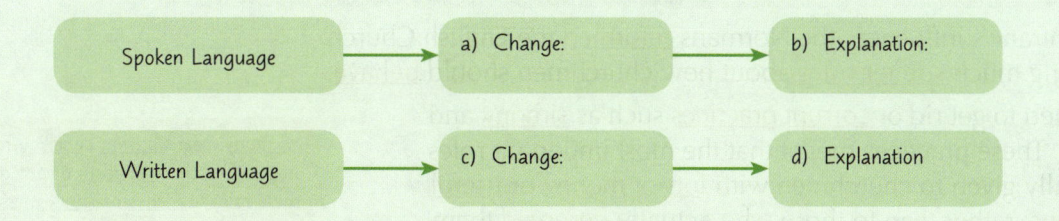

Spoken Language → a) Change: → b) Explanation:

Written Language → c) Change: → d) Explanation

2) Do you think the Norman Conquest had a significant effect on culture in England? Explain your answer.

EXAM TIP

All this change — it's hard to keep up with the Normans...
If you get a question about culture in the exam, there are lots of different aspects you could write about, from changes to language and the Church to new customs like trial by combat.

Norman England, 1066-1088

The Norman Church

William needed to maintain a close relationship with the Church, so he started to fill it with his allies...

William Replaced Anglo-Saxon Church Leaders

1) William gradually replaced the most powerful figures in the English Church (e.g. archbishops and bishops) with Norman supporters — some Anglo-Saxon churchmen were forced to leave their positions, but sometimes William waited until an Anglo-Saxon churchman stepped down and then replaced him. By 1087, only one of the bishops in England was Anglo-Saxon.

2) However, William did not replace Anglo-Saxon churchmen at lower levels — there were still a lot of Anglo-Saxon monks in 1087, and the majority of parish priests were also Anglo-Saxon.

Comment and Analysis

William needed the support of churchmen because they were powerful figures in society. They held large areas of land, played a vital role in government, and were able to influence ordinary people's opinions about the conquest and their attitudes towards the Normans.

Stigand was the Corrupt Archbishop of Canterbury

1) Stigand had been an advisor to Edward the Confessor and an ally of Harold Godwinson. He had also supported Edwin and Morcar in their attempt to place Edgar Atheling on the throne in 1066 (see p.20).

2) Stigand eventually accepted William as king, but William didn't trust him. However, it was useful for William to keep Stigand as the Archbishop of Canterbury as he could negotiate with the Anglo-Saxons. Stigand was also too powerful for William to remove him until the Norman Conquest was more secure.

3) As well as being Archbishop of Canterbury, Stigand was Bishop of Winchester. This was known as pluralism, and it was forbidden by the Church — in 1070, William let the Pope's representatives remove Stigand from office for pluralism.

4) Stigand's removal allowed William to appoint a foreign supporter, Lanfranc, as Archbishop of Canterbury. The most important man in the English Church was no longer an Anglo-Saxon, which strengthened William's control over England.

Pluralism means holding multiple religious offices.

Archbishop Lanfranc Reformed the English Church

1) Under Lanfranc's influence, the Normans reformed the English Church by imposing much stricter rules about how churchmen should behave.

2) They wanted to get rid of corrupt practices such as simony and nepotism. These practices meant that the most important roles were usually given to churchmen with lots of money or useful connections, rather than to those who actually deserved them.

Simony means buying or selling roles in the Church. Nepotism means giving these roles to friends or family members.

3) Another major problem in the English Church was clerical marriage. Churchmen were meant to remain unmarried and dedicate their lives to God, but a lot of Anglo-Saxon churchmen had wives or mistresses.

Comment and Analysis

During the 11th century, there was a widespread movement for church reform across Europe. This change started to affect England before 1066, but the Norman Conquest might have increased the speed of change by bringing new churchmen who were keen on reform.

4) To solve these issues, the Normans restructured the Church to make it more centralised. For example, the Archbishop of Canterbury was given more power and influence. This allowed Lanfranc to assert authority over churchmen and force them to obey religious laws.

5) Lanfranc also imposed discipline on the Church through the use of councils, where churchmen discussed different aspects of religious law and church life, and made important decisions.

6) Finally, Lanfranc introduced church courts to England in order to try churchmen who were accused of breaking religious laws. This gave the Church the ability to enforce good behaviour among churchmen.

Norman England, 1066-1088

The Norman Church

The appointment of Lanfranc as Archbishop of Canterbury led to many changes in the English Church during William's reign as king. Complete the activities below to help you understand these changes.

Knowledge and Understanding

1) Explain how the following churchmen were affected by the conquest:
   a) Senior churchmen like archbishops and bishops
   b) Ordinary churchmen like monks and parish priests

2) Explain what is meant by each of the following terms:

   a) Pluralism   b) Simony   c) Nepotism   d) Clerical marriage

3) Give three examples of how the Normans reformed the English Church.

4) Why might the Norman Conquest have sped up the process of Church reform in England?

Thinking Historically

1) The table below lists three statements about the Archbishops of Canterbury during William's reign as King of England. Tick the relevant box to show whether each statement applies to Stigand, Lanfranc or both. Give an explanation for each choice.

Statement	Stigand	Lanfranc	Both
a) He was against corrupt practices in the Church.			
b) He was useful to William during his time as Archbishop.			
c) He was removed from the post of Archbishop.			

2) Why do you think William trusted Lanfranc more than he trusted Stigand?

3) Why was it important for the Normans to have control over the Church?

EXAM TIP

The new Archbishop was Lanfranc about changes...

When you're writing longer answers, the prompts in the question are a great starting point for what to write about, but you need to discuss other factors as well in order to get the top marks.

Norman England, 1066-1088

Bishop Odo of Bayeux

Bishop Odo is an example of how good (and how bad) life could get for the nobility in Norman England.

Bishop Odo was King William's Half-Brother

1) In 1049, William made Odo (his half-brother) Bishop of Bayeux — a town in Normandy.
2) Odo supported William's claim to the English throne. He provided men and ships for the invasion and fought at the Battle of Hastings.
3) In return for supporting him in 1066, William made Odo Earl of Kent. William often put his supporters in positions of power to guarantee their loyalty — he had already done this in Normandy, and did it again in England in order to make his own position more secure.
4) Odo is also known for supposedly ordering the creation of the Bayeux Tapestry.

> **Comment and Analysis**
> The tapestry shows Odo advising William before the invasion and fighting bravely in the battle. However, as the tapestry was made for Odo, it's likely to exaggerate the role he played in the conquest. Even so, it's clear that he was one of William's most important and influential followers.

> The Bayeux Tapestry is one of the most important surviving sources about the Norman Conquest. The tapestry is nearly 70m long and tells the story of William's claim to the English throne and his victory over Harold Godwinson at Hastings. It was probably made to hang in Odo's cathedral in Bayeux.

He was one of the Most Powerful Men in England...

1) As Earl of Kent, Odo controlled the south east of England. This was one of the most important areas in the country, as the Normans needed to maintain control of the crossing to Normandy.
2) Being Earl of Kent made Odo very rich and powerful. According to Domesday Book, he had estates in twenty-two counties. This meant he controlled more land than any other Norman earl in England.
3) In 1067, William returned to Normandy and named a few trusted followers as his regents (see p.38), including Odo. As regent, Odo used harsh measures against the Anglo-Saxons to keep them under control. This might have made them more hostile to the Normans.

> The 12th-century writer Orderic Vitalis is critical of Odo, saying that he was cruel and destructive.

> **Comment and Analysis**
> Odo treated the Anglo-Saxons harshly, but the Normans might have seen it as necessary in order to maintain control over the newly-conquered country. His actions helped to secure William's authority in England in the first years of the conquest.

...but his Greed and Ambition made him Unpopular

1) As soon as he became Earl of Kent, Odo started seizing large amounts of land and wealth from the landowners in the earldom, either taking it for himself or giving it to his supporters. This made him unpopular with the people of Kent.
2) In 1067, there was a rebellion against Odo. The people of Kent attempted to capture Dover Castle with the support of a foreign lord (Eustace of Boulogne) but they failed.
3) Odo's behaviour caused conflict with Archbishop Lanfranc of Canterbury (see p.48), who also held land in the south east. In the 1070s, Odo was tried in court after being accused of taking land that belonged to the Church. He was ordered to give up some of the lands he had gained.
4) Odo's ambition eventually led to his downfall. In 1082, he gathered troops and planned a journey to Italy. The sources give different explanations for this journey, but some say that he was trying to make himself the Pope. William arrested and imprisoned him, and he was only released after William died.

> Some sources suggest that William disliked the way Odo governed the land that he'd been given, and only arrested him to get rid of him.

Norman England, 1066-1088

Bishop Odo of Bayeux

SKILLS PRACTICE

Odo played an important role during William's reign as King of England, but he also upset many people with his actions. Try the activities on this page to see if you know about the highs and lows of Odo of Bayeux.

Knowledge and Understanding

1) Copy and complete the timeline below about Odo's rise and fall in power.
   Fill in all the key events between 1049 and 1082, giving as much detail as possible.

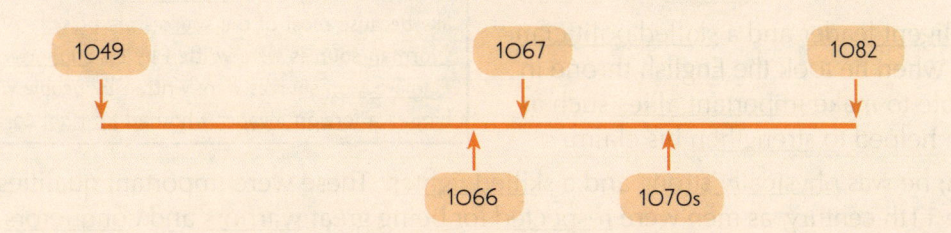

   1049 — 1066 — 1067 — 1070s — 1082

2) What were Odo's responsibilities as Earl of Kent?

3) Explain why there was a rebellion against Odo during his time as Earl of Kent.

Thinking Historically

1) In your own words, explain why Bishop Odo can be considered a significant figure in Norman England. You can use the factors in the boxes below to help you write your answer.

   - Odo's role in the Battle of Hastings
   - Odo's role in securing England
   - Odo's conflict with important figures

2) What does Odo's reign as Earl of Kent suggest about how secure the power of earls was during William's reign? Explain your answer.

3) In your own words, explain how each of the following factors may have contributed to Odo losing power.
   a) Odo taking land that belonged to the Church.
   b) Odo gathering troops to take to Italy.
   c) The way Odo governed his lands.

EXAM TIP

Ambitious is one word for trying to make yourself Pope...

Sometimes in history, it's not clear exactly what happened or why it happened, e.g. Odo's planned journey to Italy. Using phrases like 'some sources say' is a good way to show this.

Norman England, 1066-1088

William I and Robert Curthose

William the Conqueror is one of the most famous Kings of England, but not everyone can agree on whether or not he was a good one. It's safe to say that William's eldest son, Robert Curthose, wasn't his biggest fan...

William is Praised and Criticised by Different Sources

1) William maintained control over Normandy and England despite many challenges to his rule in both territories. This shows his strength as a leader.

2) He was an intelligent leader and a skilled politician — for example, when he took the English throne in 1066, he was able to make important allies such as the Pope, which helped to strengthen his claim.

Comment and Analysis

It's difficult to get an accurate idea of what William was like because most of the sources are biased. Most of the Norman sources were written by his supporters, whereas Anglo-Saxon sources were written by people who viewed him as a foreign invader who had no right to be their king.

3) As a young man, he was physically strong and a skilled fighter. These were important qualities for a ruler in the 11th century, as men were respected for being great warriors and conquerors.

4) William was very religious. He made large donations to churches and cathedrals and oversaw the construction of new monasteries. Even Anglo-Saxons praised William for being a devoted Christian.

5) However, the way William is presented in certain sources has led some historians to view him as cruel. The Anglo-Saxon Chronicle criticises him for oppressing the English. Even William of Poitiers (a Norman) was shocked by the brutal killing of Anglo-Saxons at the Battle of Hastings and during the Harrying of the North.

6) William is often seen as greedy. He took a lot of wealth from the Anglo-Saxons through taxation and was extremely unpopular for setting aside large areas of the kingdom as royal forest (see p.40).

Robert Curthose wanted to be Duke of Normandy

1) In the later years of William's reign, his eldest son (Robert Curthose) started to demand more authority. Robert had been named as William's successor in Normandy, but he wouldn't receive any real authority until William died. Robert resented William for preventing him from gaining wealth and power.

2) In the late 1070s, Robert asked William to let him rule Normandy while William ruled England — William refused. This caused an argument, and Robert went into exile in order to start a rebellion.

Robert's nickname ('Curthose') means 'short boots'. He was probably given this name to make fun of his height.

3) Robert gathered his forces at Gerberoy, near the border between Normandy and the rest of France. He raided the surrounding area, forcing William to meet him in battle.

4) Robert won the battle. This was a humiliating defeat for William, and it showed that Robert was a serious threat. Many people advised William to reconcile with Robert:

- Robert was supported by the sons of many Norman lords. These lords wanted to end the problems between William and Robert to avoid their families losing favour with the king.
- Matilda (William's wife and Robert's mother) tried to get William to forgive their son. She also sent Robert money during his exile, against her husband's wishes.

5) William eventually allowed Robert to return to Normandy and confirmed that he would inherit Normandy when William died. However, Robert didn't receive the power he wanted during his father's lifetime. He eventually went back into exile, where he remained until his father's death.

Norman England, 1066-1088

William I and Robert Curthose

While William was trying to stabilise his position in England, he was also trying to keep his home and family under control. See if you have William and Robert's relationship covered with these activities.

Knowledge and Understanding

1) Why do the sources about William's life make it difficult to know what he was really like?

2) In your own words, explain why Robert rebelled against William.

3) Copy and complete the flowchart below, filling in the missing events during Robert's rebellion against his father. Give as much detail as possible.

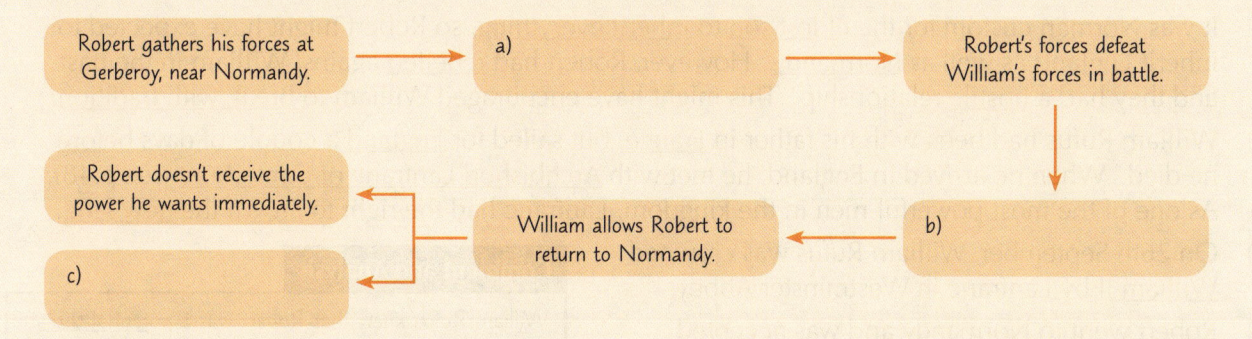

- Robert gathers his forces at Gerberoy, near Normandy. → a) → Robert's forces defeat William's forces in battle.
- Robert doesn't receive the power he wants immediately. ← William allows Robert to return to Normandy. ← b)
- c) ←

4) Why was it significant that Robert defeated William in battle?

Thinking Historically

1) Some people believe that William was a cruel king. Use the table to help you structure each paragraph of an essay, explaining how far you agree with this view. Each row should represent a paragraph of your essay. You can use other pages from this section to help you fill in your table.

Point	Evidence	Why evidence supports point
William made life very difficult for many Anglo-Saxon peasants.	William introduced the royal forest, an area of land reserved as hunting grounds for the king. There were restrictions on how peasants could use land in the royal forest.	The royal forest meant there was less land for peasants to use for hunting and gathering food. This suggests William was a cruel king who didn't care about the wellbeing of his subjects.

- Add three rows to the table to structure three more paragraphs.
- Make sure you write points that agree and disagree with the statement.
- Talk about different factors that relate to the question.

EXAM TIP: *William couldn't deal with his son's rebellious nature...*
Individuals like William had an impact over a long period — you should know how Norman England changed over time to understand why William changed his policies during his reign.

Norman England, 1066-1088

The Death of William I

William I ruled England and Normandy, but when he died these lands were split between two of his sons — Robert Curthose and William Rufus. Unfortunately, the brothers weren't very good at sharing...

There was a Dispute over the Succession when William Died

1) In 1087, William was at war with the King of France over some land on the border of Normandy. While his army was attacking Mantes (a town in northern France), William was seriously injured.
2) William died a few weeks later on 9th September 1087. His sons inherited his lands and wealth:

   - His eldest son, Robert Curthose (see p.52), became Duke of Normandy.
   - His second son, William Rufus, became King of England.
   - His youngest son, Henry, was given £5000 — a huge amount of money.

3) It was Norman custom for the eldest son to inherit everything, so Robert might have expected to inherit England as well as Normandy. However, Robert had rebelled against William in the past and they had a hostile relationship. This might have encouraged William to break with tradition.
4) William Rufus had been with his father in France, but sailed for England a couple of days before he died. When he arrived in England, he met with Archbishop Lanfranc of Canterbury (see p.48). As one of the most powerful men in the kingdom, Lanfranc had the right to crown the new king.
5) On 26th September, William Rufus was crowned William II by Lanfranc in Westminster Abbey.
6) Robert went to Normandy and was accepted as duke. However, he believed that William had wrongfully seized the throne of England.

> **Comment and Analysis**
>
> William Rufus knew that Robert was a potential threat. By acting quickly and gaining the support of Lanfranc, William Rufus was able to secure the English throne.

There was a Rebellion against William II taking the Throne

1) Robert wasn't the only one who believed William Rufus shouldn't be King of England. Many Norman lords also believed that, as the eldest son, Robert should have inherited England as well as Normandy.
2) Many lords held land in England and Normandy, meaning they had to serve both William and Robert. This was difficult because William and Robert disliked each other. The lords thought their lives would be easier if Normandy and England were united under one ruler.
3) Odo of Bayeux (see p.50), the king's uncle, led a rebellion against William Rufus in 1088. William had released Odo from prison and restored his lands to him as soon as he became king, but Odo still wanted to make Robert the King of England instead.

> Odo and the other lords believed Robert would be easier to control than William, allowing them to increase their own power and influence. Odo was particularly keen to regain the power that he had possessed before his imprisonment in 1082.

4) Odo and his allies planned to overthrow William by gaining the support of more lords and securing the south coast. This would have allowed the rebels to bring reinforcements from Normandy.
5) However, most of the lords in England were loyal to William — Odo wasn't able to gather enough support for the rebellion. Robert remained in Normandy and didn't supply his supporters with the reinforcements they needed. The rebellion failed and William sent Odo into exile for his betrayal.

William II was an Unpopular King

1) William II was viewed as a harsh and greedy king. He took a lot of money from the English through taxation and he also gained a lot of wealth from the Church.
2) He continued to fight against Robert until 1096, when Robert gave Normandy to William. This meant that William was in control of both Normandy and England.
3) In 1100, William was killed in a hunting accident. His younger brother Henry became King of England.

Norman England, 1066-1088

The Death of William I

Many people disagreed over who should be King of England after William I's death. The activities below will help you understand why these disagreements happened and the consequences they had.

Knowledge and Understanding

1) What did each of William I's sons inherit from him?

2) Using the key words and phrases below, explain how William Rufus was able to secure his position as King of England in 1087.

   William I   sailed for England   quickly   Archbishop Lanfranc

3) Copy and complete the timeline below about William II's reign as King of England. Fill in all of the key events between 1087 and 1100, giving as much detail as possible.

   9th Sept 1087 — 1088 — 1100
   26th Sept 1087 — 1096

4) In your own words, explain how Odo planned to overthrow William II.

5) Why did Odo's rebellion fail? Explain your answer.

Thinking Historically

1) Explain why the following people were unhappy with the way William I's lands were divided up after his death.

People	Why they were unhappy with the division of land
a) Robert Curthose	
b) Odo of Bayeux	
c) Norman lords	

EXAM TIP

William II — the cash grab sequel to William I...
Make sure the points you make in an answer are relevant to the question — you could write about William II for a question about the succession in 1087, but not for one about Hastings.

Norman England, 1066-1088

Worked Exam-Style Question

The sample answer below should give you some advice for answering the 16-mark question in the exam.

'The main reason Robert Curthose failed to become King of England was a lack of support.'

Explain how far you agree with this statement.

You could mention:
- Robert's relationship with William I
- Odo of Bayeux

You should also use your own knowledge.   [16 marks]

The prompts in the question are only there as a guide. To get a high mark, you'll also need to include ideas of your own that go beyond the prompts.

This directly addresses the question in the first sentence.

I agree that the main reason Robert Curthose failed to become King of England was a lack of support. While Robert's failure to take decisive action also contributed to his failure to become king, it was the lack of support from his father, Archbishop Lanfranc and the nobility which ultimately stopped Robert from taking the throne.

This gives a summary of the overall argument.

This refers back to the question wording.

Robert's failure to gain his father's support was a key reason why he did not become King of England, because William I did not name Robert as his successor in England. According to Norman custom, the eldest son inherited everything from his father, so Robert might have expected to become King of England as well as Duke of Normandy when William I died. However, Robert and William had a hostile relationship. For example, Robert had rebelled against William in the 1070s when William I refused to share power and allow Robert to rule Normandy. This may have led William I to break with tradition and not leave everything to Robert. William I's lack of support for Robert therefore contributed to Robert's failure to become King of England as it gave William Rufus the opportunity to establish himself as king instead.

This links the information back to the question and analyses a reason for Robert's failure to take the English throne.

Robert's lack of support from Archbishop Lanfranc was another reason why he did not become king. This was significant because Lanfranc was the most powerful churchman in England and had the right to crown the new king. Instead of supporting Robert, Lanfranc crowned William Rufus as king, which implied that William II's rule was backed by the Church and by God. As a result, people were encouraged to support William II's claim to the throne, which helped him gain loyal followers in England. Lanfranc's decision to back William Rufus instead of Robert put Robert at a disadvantage when trying to claim the throne.

This explains how and why Lanfranc's support of William II affected Robert negatively.

Norman England, 1066-1088

Worked Exam-Style Question

The lack of support for Robert among the nobility was another important reason why he did not become King of England. Although Odo of Bayeux led a rebellion in 1088 which aimed to overthrow William II and put Robert on the throne, lack of support for Robert meant that the rebellion failed. Odo planned to gain enough support to control the south coast of England so he could secure a passage for reinforcements from Normandy. However, Odo was unable to achieve this because the majority of the lords in England remained loyal to William II.

While a lack of support was a key reason why Robert did not become King of England, Robert's lack of decisive action to claim the throne was also important. After William I's death, Robert went to Normandy to be accepted as duke, but he did not immediately make a claim on England. In contrast, William Rufus acted swiftly by sailing to England a couple of days before William I's death on 9th September and meeting with Lanfranc. This enabled William Rufus to be crowned king on 26th September. Robert also failed to act decisively during Odo's rebellion in 1088. He did not come to England or send reinforcements to support the rebellion, and this contributed to the rebellion's failure. Due to Robert's lack of decisive action, William Rufus was able to establish himself as King of England with limited opposition. However, even if Robert had acted more decisively, the lack of support from key figures like Lanfranc and the nobility would have made it very difficult for him to claim the throne. Therefore, Robert's lack of action was not the most important reason why he failed to become king.

Overall, a lack of support was the main reason why Robert Curthose did not become King of England. The fact that neither William I nor Lanfranc gave their support to Robert meant that William Rufus was able to claim the throne. Furthermore, the lack of support from the nobility made it difficult for Robert to dethrone his brother. Although Robert's lack of decisive action contributed to his failure to become king, ultimately the lack of support from the most powerful figures in England prevented him from claiming the throne.

Annotations:
- Use **relevant details** to **support** your points.
- Even if you agree with the statement, it's important to look at **other factors** — this shows that you've considered **alternative arguments**.
- This introduces a **factor** that **isn't a prompt** from the question.
- Use **accurate details** from your **own knowledge** to **back up** your points.
- This compares **different factors** and explains why one is **more important** than the others.
- Make sure you end by **clearly stating** your opinion in the **conclusion**.
- This **sums up** why a lack of support was the **most important** reason why Robert didn't become king.

Norman England, 1066-1088

Exam-Style Questions

Use your knowledge of the Normans to help you answer these exam-style questions. If there are any pages in this section that you're not very confident about, take another look at those before you start.

Exam-Style Questions

1) Describe two aspects of the royal forest. [4 marks]

2) Explain why the English Church changed under William I.

   You could mention:
   - corruption
   - Archbishop Lanfranc

   You should also use your own knowledge. [12 marks]

3) 'The main consequence of the Norman Conquest for the government of England was the increased power of the sheriffs.'

   To what extent do you agree with this statement? Explain your answer.

   You could mention:
   - the royal demesne
   - writs

   You should also use your own knowledge. [16 marks]

Norman England, 1066-1088

Answers

Marking the Activities

We've included sample answers for all the activities. When you're marking your work, remember that our answers are just a guide — a lot of activities ask you to give your own opinion, so there isn't always a 'correct answer'.

Marking the Exam-Style Questions

For each exam-style question, we've covered some key points that your answer could include.
Our answers are just examples though — answers very different to ours could also get top marks.

Most exam questions in history are level marked. This means the examiner puts your answer into one of several levels. Then they award marks based on how well your answer matches the description for that level.

To reach a higher level, you'll need to give a 'more sophisticated' answer. Exactly what 'sophisticated' means will depend on the type of question, but, generally speaking, a more sophisticated answer could include more detail, more background knowledge or make a more complex judgement.

Here's how to use levels to mark your answers:

1. Start by choosing which level your answer falls into.
   - Pick the level description that your answer matches most closely. If different parts of your answer match different level descriptions, then pick the level description that best matches your answer as a whole.
   - To do this, start at 'Level 1' and go to the next level if your answer meets all the conditions of a level. E.g. choose 'Level 3' if your answer meets all the conditions for 'Level 3' and a few of the conditions for 'Level 4'.

2. Now you need to choose a mark — look at the range of marks that are available within the level you've chosen.
   - If your answer completely matches the level description, or parts of it match the level above, then give yourself a high mark within the range of the level.
   - If your answer mostly matches the level description, but some parts of it only just match, then give yourself a mark in the middle of the range.
   - Award yourself a lower mark within the range if your answer only just meets the conditions for that level.

The 4-mark exam-style questions aren't level marked, so the mark schemes for these questions are given on the relevant page of the answers.

Level Descriptions:

12-Mark Questions:

Level 1
1-3 marks
Limited knowledge of the period is shown. The answer gives one or more simple explanations and demonstrates only a limited understanding of causation. Ideas are generally unconnected and don't follow a logical order.

Level 2
4-6 marks
Some relevant knowledge and understanding of the period is shown. The answer gives a basic analysis of the topic and demonstrates a basic understanding of causation. An attempt has been made to organise ideas in a logical way.

Level 3
7-9 marks
A good level of knowledge and understanding of the period is shown. The answer explores multiple explanations and demonstrates a good understanding of causation. It identifies some relevant connections between different points, and ideas are organised logically.

Level 4
10-12 marks
Answers can't be awarded Level 4 if they only discuss the information suggested in the question. Knowledge and understanding of the period is precise and detailed. The answer considers a range of explanations and demonstrates a clear understanding of causation. All ideas are organised logically. Connections between different points are identified to create a developed analysis of the topic.

16-Mark Questions:

Level 1
1-4 marks
The answer shows limited knowledge and understanding of the period. It gives a simple explanation of one or more factors relating to the topic. Ideas aren't organised with an overall argument in mind. There is no clear conclusion.

Level 2
5-8 marks
The answer shows some appropriate knowledge and understanding of the period. There is some analysis of how different factors relate to the topic. Ideas are organised with an overall argument in mind, but the conclusion isn't well supported by the answer.

Level 3
9-12 marks
The answer shows a good level of knowledge and understanding of the period, which is relevant to the question. It analyses how several different factors relate to the topic. Most ideas are organised to develop a clear argument that supports the conclusion.

Level 4
13-16 marks
Answers can't be awarded Level 4 if they only discuss the information suggested in the question. The answer shows an excellent level of relevant knowledge and understanding of the period. It analyses in detail how a range of factors relate to the topic. All ideas are well organised to develop a clear argument and a well-supported conclusion.

Answers

Anglo-Saxon England and the Norman Conquest, 1060-1066

Page 5 — Anglo-Saxon Society and Government

Knowledge and Understanding

1
- King — He was the wealthiest and most powerful person in society. He was expected to protect the country from invaders and run the kingdom as the head of the government. He needed the support of the nobility to run the country.
- Earls — They were the most powerful noblemen. They governed large areas of land called earldoms, which were given to them by the king.
- Thegns — They were less powerful members of the nobility who received smaller areas of land from their lord. Sheriffs were usually thegns.
- Peasants and Slaves — Peasant farmers made up the majority of the population. They were given a plot of land in return for doing agricultural work for their lord. Some peasants were slaves who were labourers that could be bought and sold.

2 Churchmen were important to Anglo-Saxon government because they could read and write, so they could create written records to help the king manage his kingdom. They were also a part of the Witan and helped to advise the king.

3 a) The king's council, made up of powerful nobles and high-ranking churchmen, who advised the king and helped him govern the kingdom.
  b) A smaller area of land within an earldom, which was controlled by a sheriff.
  c) A smaller area of land within a shire, which contained multiple villages and was controlled by a sheriff and his deputy.

4 Here are some points your mind map may include:
- The king assigned earls and sheriffs to govern their own shires and hundreds. This meant that the king had support in running the whole country, which allowed him to oversee the kingdom as head of the government.
- The king was advised by the Witan, a council of powerful nobles and high-ranking churchmen. This meant the king had a range of advisors to help him make decisions.
- The Anglo-Saxons kept written government records, which helped them to run the country effectively.
- The tax system was highly organised. The amount of tax owed was based on the value of each shire's land.

5 Earls and sheriffs were expected to organise and lead the fyrd (the region's fighting force) into battle when the king summoned them. They also made sure taxes were collected within their lands. They were responsible for running the local courts and bringing criminals to justice — earls oversaw shire courts and sheriffs ran hundred courts.

Page 7 — Life in Anglo-Saxon England

Knowledge and Understanding

1 Villages:
- They were occupied by peasants or slaves.
- Most people lived in villages.
- They were governed by a thegn.
- Farming was important for the economy of a village.
- Peasants and slaves in villages mostly worked the land.
- Parish churches were often built in villages.

Towns:
- A small minority of the population lived in towns.
- They were centres of business and commerce.
- A variety of people, such as craftsmen and merchants, lived in towns.
- Parish churches were often built in towns.

2 People at the top of the social hierarchy could become rich and influential. People at the bottom of the hierarchy were often poor and didn't have much control over their lives, which made it difficult for them to improve their situation.

3 The Church was split up into sixteen dioceses. Each diocese was controlled by a bishop. Dioceses were starting to be divided into parishes by 1066.

4
- Ordinary people attended mass performed by a priest.
- The Church carried out ceremonies for ordinary people, such as baptisms and burials.
- Ordinary people confessed their sins and did penance before a priest.

Thinking Historically

1 Church:
- It received gifts such as land and precious objects.
- It received protection from violence and robbery.
- It sometimes received the second-born sons of the nobility to train as priests, which helped the Church to grow.

Nobility:
- They sent their second-born sons to train as priests, which reduced competition for land within the nobility.

Answers

- They had influence over the appointment of bishops, abbots and priests, meaning they could give important posts to their relatives and followers.
- The Church said prayers for the nobility. The nobility believed prayers would help them get into heaven and have success on earth.

2. You can answer either way, as long as you explain your answer. For example:
   - The nobility were more important because they helped the king maintain control over the whole of the country. The earls were responsible for governing their earldoms and dealt with most issues in their own lands, such as enforcing law and order and organising the fyrd when the king required it. They were also part of the Witan, which meant they helped the king govern the country.
   - The Church was more important because it helped the king govern by legitimising his claim to the throne. The Church's support suggested that the king also had God's support. This made the king's position more secure. High-ranking churchmen also had a role on the Witan and gave advice to the king. Churchmen could read and write, meaning they could keep records for the king that were needed to manage the kingdom.

Page 9 — The House of Godwin

Knowledge and Understanding

1. a) The King of England from 1042 to 1066.
   b) The Earl of Wessex from 1018, making him one of the most powerful men in England.
   c) Godwin's son. He was Earl of East Anglia and then became Earl of Wessex when his father died.
   d) Godwin's son and Harold's brother. He was Earl of Northumbria.
   e) Godwin's daughter. She was King Edward's wife and the Queen of England.
   f) Two of Godwin's sons. They were also earls in England.

2.
   - 1018 — Godwin becomes Earl of Wessex, making him earl of the oldest and richest earldom in the kingdom.
   - 1042 — Edward becomes King of England, and his claim to the throne is backed by Godwin.
   - 1051 — Godwin rebels against the king. He is outlawed by Edward and flees the country with his family.
   - 1052 — Godwin returns to England with a large army, demanding to be restored as Earl of Wessex. Edward gives in because he doesn't have enough support to fight Godwin. He makes Godwin Earl of Wessex again.
   - 1053 — Godwin dies and his son Harold is made Earl of Wessex. This makes Harold the most powerful man in England except for King Edward.

Thinking Historically

1. a)
   - The Godwins held a lot of land across the country and so controlled large areas of the kingdom. For example, Harold was Earl of Wessex and Tostig was Earl of Northumbria, two of the largest earldoms in England.
   - The Godwins' large share of land meant they were very wealthy.
   - The Godwins gave land to their allies to gain support.

   b)
   - The Godwins' wealth allowed them to acquire and maintain a large number of followers. They were also able to grant gifts to their allies, ensuring their loyalty and support.
   - The Godwins used their wealth to pay skilled fighters to join their household.

   c)
   - Godwin's military strength allowed him to regain his position as Earl of Wessex in 1052 after he was exiled.
   - Harold and Tostig were able to defeat threats to England — for example, they fought and defeated a rebellious Welsh king in 1063.

2. a) Evidence for — Harold made sure that Tostig became Earl of Northumbria instead of someone from a rival family gaining the earldom. This strengthened the Godwins' position in the kingdom.
   Evidence against — The Godwin family became powerful because of Godwin's rise in social status. Godwin's intelligence and political skill enabled him to rise from the lower nobility and gain an earldom.

   b) Evidence for — Edward outlawed Godwin in 1051 when Godwin's rebellion against the king failed. This shows Edward had the ability to take away the Godwins' power.
   Evidence against — Godwin demanded to be restored as Earl of Wessex in 1052 and Edward gave in to his demands. This suggests that Godwin's military strength gave him power over Edward.

   c) Evidence for — Harold had a strong relationship with Stigand, the Archbishop of Canterbury. Having the support of an important churchman made Harold's position more secure.
   Evidence against — Harold was able to use his wealth to attract and maintain followers, which was an important factor in securing his power.

Answers

Page 11 — Harold, Tostig and King Edward

Knowledge and Understanding

1. Norman sources:
   - Harold was sent to Normandy by Edward to name William as the heir to the English throne.
   - Harold swore an oath to support William's claim to the throne.

   English sources:
   - Some sources say Harold went to Normandy to secure the release of his brother and nephew, who were hostages there.
   - Other sources suggest he had been shipwrecked in northern France during a fishing trip.
   - The sources suggest that Harold swore an oath to William, but some say that William forced him to do it.

2. The Norman sources supported William's claim by suggesting that Edward had promised him the throne. This made him seem like Edward's rightful successor. They also undermined Harold's claim to the throne by suggesting he had promised to support William's claim.

3. a) • Tostig was unpopular with the people of Northumbria because he had raised taxes in the area. He had also ordered the murder of several local noblemen.
   b) • The Northumbrians rebelled against Tostig and killed many of his supporters. They also demanded that Morcar be appointed earl.
   • King Edward sent Harold to deal with the rebels and support Tostig. Instead, Harold appointed Morcar as earl and sent Tostig into exile.

Thinking Historically

1. Tostig was Earl of Northumbria, making him a powerful earl and a potential threat to Harold's power — the rebellion against Tostig allowed Harold to remove a potential rival. Harold also managed to gain a powerful ally in Morcar by helping him become the new Earl of Northumbria.

2. a) Edward's mother was a daughter of the Duke of Normandy, meaning that Edward had relatives in Normandy.
   b) Three of the Kings of England before Edward had been Scandinavians. This meant there were people from this region who felt they had a claim to the throne.

Page 13 — Claimants to the Throne in 1066

Knowledge and Understanding

1. a) Harold Godwinson was the most powerful nobleman in England. He was very ambitious and wanted to become king to secure his authority.
   b) William was the Duke of Normandy. He wanted to become king because it would make him more powerful and give him the same high status as the King of France. It would also make him wealthier as England was a rich country.
   c) Harald Hardrada was the King of Norway. He wanted to take back the empire that had belonged to King Cnut, a former Scandinavian ruler of England.

2. Being related to the king was an important factor that could give someone a strong claim to the throne. Military strength was also an important factor as a claimant needed to be able to take control of the country.

Thinking Historically

1. a) Strengths:
   - Edgar was related to King Edward.

   Weaknesses:
   - He was only a teenager.
   - He hadn't proven himself as a leader.

   b) Strengths:
   - Harold was the most powerful nobleman in England.
   - He was close to the royal family. His father, Godwin, had helped Edward become king, and his sister, Edith, was the queen.
   - Harold claimed Edward had asked him to be king on his deathbed.
   - Harold was an experienced military leader.

   Weaknesses:
   - He wasn't related to Edward.
   - He had supposedly made an oath to support William's claim to the throne.

   c) Strengths:
   - William was a powerful and successful military leader.
   - Some sources claim that Edward had promised William the throne, and Harold had sworn to support his claim.
   - He had a lot of experience as a ruler.
   - The Pope supported his claim, suggesting God was on his side.
   - He was related to Edward.

   Weaknesses:
   - There was uncertainty about whether Edward had promised him the throne.

Answers

   d) Strengths:
- Harald was an experienced ruler.
- He was known for his military prowess.

   Weaknesses:
- He claimed he was heir to England's Scandinavian kings, rather than to Edward.

2 You can choose any of the claimants, as long as you explain your answer. For example:
William had the strongest claim to the throne in 1066. He was related to Edward and was also a skilled military leader who had great success in stabilising Normandy in the past. This made him a more suitable leader than Edgar, who had no military experience. Although other claimants also had military experience, such as Harold and Hardrada, neither of them were related to Edward.

3 You can choose any of the claimants, as long as you explain your answer. For example:
Edgar Atheling had the weakest claim to the throne. Although he was related to Edward, he had no military experience or experience of ruling a kingdom. Other claimants who were related to Edward, such as William, had more experience than Edgar.

Page 15 — The Struggle for the Throne

Knowledge and Understanding

1 a) A part-time military force made up of ordinary people. They could be summoned away from their normal work when the king required men to fight and only served for two months at a time.
  b) A professional, highly trained warrior.

2 The Witan selected Harold as successor to Edward because they thought he was the best leader to protect the country from invasion.

3
- January 1066 — Edward dies and Harold is crowned King of England.
- Mid-1066 — Harold is prepared for an invasion. He and his army wait to defend the south coast of England against a Norman invasion.
- Early September 1066 — Supplies start to run low and the fyrd need to return home to collect the harvest. Harold dismisses the fyrd and returns to London. Soon after, Harald Hardrada and Tostig invade north-eastern England.
- 20th September 1066 — Earls Edwin and Morcar fight Hardrada at the Battle of Gate Fulford. The Anglo-Saxon forces are defeated and Hardrada gains a foothold in the north of England.
- 25th September 1066 — Harold defeats Hardrada at the Battle of Stamford Bridge. Hardrada and Tostig are killed, as is a large part of their army. The rest of the defeated army withdraws.

Thinking Historically

1 a) The Anglo-Saxons lost.
- The Anglo-Saxon leaders Edwin and Morcar were inexperienced compared to Hardrada, who was an experienced military leader.
- The Scandinavian army were more experienced fighters than the Anglo-Saxon army.

  b) The Anglo-Saxons won.
- Harold's army consisted of professional fighters, the housecarls.
- Harold's fast march north meant he took Hardrada and the Scandinavian army by surprise — this gave him an advantage in the battle.

2 Harold defeated the Scandinavians at the Battle of Stamford Bridge and Hardrada was killed in the battle. This meant Harold had removed Hardrada as one of his main rivals to the throne and strengthened his own position as king. However, there were also negative consequences of the battle. Many of Harold's troops had been killed, and those who were still alive were tired from the quick march north. In addition to this, Harold and his army were in the north when the Normans invaded the south coast of England. This meant Harold was at a disadvantage when the Normans arrived.

Page 17 — The Battle of Hastings

Knowledge and Understanding

1
- The Normans couldn't cross the English Channel until September due to poor sailing conditions.
- It's possible William knew about Hardrada's invasion, so he waited until Harold had gone north and left the south coast undefended.

2 The Normans arrived only a few days after the Battle of Stamford Bridge. This meant that the Anglo-Saxon army was in the north and had to quickly march south to face the Norman threat. This gave the Normans an advantage, because the Anglo-Saxon soldiers were weakened and exhausted from the battle and the march and didn't have much time to recover. It also meant that Harold didn't have time to gather all of his troops, so his army wasn't as large as it could have been.

3 a) The Norman army attacks the Anglo-Saxons, but they're unable to break through the shield wall.
  b) Some of the Anglo-Saxons chase the fleeing Normans, weakening the shield wall.
  c) Harold and his brothers Gyrth and Leofwine are killed. The Anglo-Saxon army is defeated.

Answers

Thinking Historically

1. Similarities:
   - Both armies were led by experienced military leaders.
   - Both armies had foot-soldiers.
   - Both armies included professional fighters — the Norman army was made up entirely of professional fighters and the Anglo-Saxons had the housecarls.

   Differences:
   - The Anglo-Saxon army was only made up of troops who fought on foot. The Norman army featured archers, who could fight from a distance, and cavalry, who could attack swiftly on horseback.
   - The Anglo-Saxon army included the fyrd, who weren't as experienced or disciplined as the professional Norman army.
   - The Anglo-Saxon army was exhausted from fighting the Battle of Stamford Bridge and then marching south to face the Normans. The Norman army was much fresher.

2. You can answer either way, as long as you explain your answer. For example:
   - William's leadership had more of an impact on the outcome of the Battle of Hastings than Harold's mistakes. William used clever tactics such as the feigned flight technique to break down the Anglo-Saxon shield wall. Despite Harold's mistake of rushing into battle too soon, the Anglo-Saxon army managed to repel the Norman attack until the Normans used the feigned flight tactic. This shows that feigned flight turned the battle in the Normans' favour, therefore William's leadership affected the battle in the most significant way.
   - Harold's mistakes had more of an impact on the outcome of the Battle of Hastings. Harold rushed into battle without taking the time to gather all of his troops and without giving his soldiers time to recover from the Battle of Stamford Bridge. This meant that he chose to fight with a weakened army rather than waiting for reinforcements to arrive and allowing his troops to rest, which meant that the Anglo-Saxons were at a disadvantage before the battle began.

Page 19 — Exam-Style Questions

1. Each aspect is marked separately and you can have a maximum of two marks per aspect. How to grade your answer:
   - 1 mark for describing one credible aspect of the legal system in Anglo-Saxon England.
   - 2 marks for describing one credible aspect of the legal system in Anglo-Saxon England and using your own knowledge to support it.

   Here are some points your answer may include:
   - The shire courts dealt with serious cases, such as criminal cases and cases that involved land and property.
   - The hundred courts tried people who were suspected of committing minor offences. For example, offences like failing to repay small debts or stealing livestock were tried in hundred courts.
   - A range of punishments, such as fines and the death penalty, were used to punish crimes. The punishment of a crime depended on how serious the crime was.

2. This question is level marked. You should look at the level descriptions on page 59 to help you mark your answer.

   Here are some points your answer may include:
   - Edward the Confessor didn't have any children, which meant there was no clear successor to the throne. This created an opportunity for lots of people with claims to the throne to try and become King of England after Edward's death.
   - Harold Godwinson believed he had a claim to the throne, which contributed to the uncertainty over the succession. He was the most powerful nobleman in England and he claimed that Edward had promised him the throne on his deathbed. This gave him a strong claim to the throne. However, according to some sources, he had previously sworn an oath to support William of Normandy's claim to the throne, which undermined his own claim.
   - William of Normandy believed he was Edward's rightful successor. William was related to Edward, and it was claimed that Edward had promised him the throne and Harold had sworn an oath to support his claim. However, there were conflicting accounts about whether Harold had sworn the oath willingly or whether William had forced him to swear it. This made it unclear whether Edward had wanted William to succeed him.
   - Some people believed Edgar Atheling should be king, but he failed to get enough support for his claim. He was related to King Edward, which helped his chances of becoming king, but he was only a teenager and didn't have any experience leading a country or an army. This made it difficult for him to get support for his claim from important nobles and the Witan.

Answers

- There were Scandinavian claimants to the throne who believed they had the right to rule. There had been three Scandinavian kings who had ruled England between 1013 and 1042. Harald Hardrada, the King of Norway, believed he was the successor to these kings. This led him to make a claim on the English throne.

3 This question is level marked. You should look at the level descriptions on page 59 to help you mark your answer.

   Here are some points your answer may include:
   - William's use of cavalry was an important reason why the Normans won the Battle of Hastings. The riders were highly skilled and disciplined, and could fight with greater speed and strength than the Anglo-Saxon foot soldiers. This allowed them to kill many Anglo-Saxon soldiers once their shield wall was broken, giving William an important advantage in the battle.
   - One of the reasons William won the Battle of Hastings was his choice of tactics. The Anglo-Saxon shield wall was initially successful at stopping the Norman army, including their cavalry, from breaking through. However, the Normans' use of feigned flight broke down the Anglo-Saxons' shield wall. This clever tactic was an important reason William won because it allowed the cavalry to be effective and turned the battle in William's favour.
   - The Anglo-Saxon army's lack of discipline was an important reason William won the Battle of Hastings. Parts of the Anglo-Saxon army, such as the fyrd, were less disciplined and less experienced than the Norman army. They left the shield wall to chase fleeing Normans rather than holding their position. This lack of discipline weakened the Anglo-Saxon army and contributed to William winning the battle.
   - Harold's decision to rush into battle contributed to William's victory. Harold immediately marched south after defeating Harald Hardrada at the Battle of Stamford Bridge and only spent a few days in London before fighting the Normans. As a result, there wasn't enough time for his soldiers to recover or for him to gather all of his troops. Harold's choice to rush his soldiers into battle meant William's fresh troops had an advantage over the tired and weakened Anglo-Saxons.
   - William won because Harold's army contained the fyrd. The fyrd was a part-time army that only served for two months at a time. After standing guard on the south coast all summer, the fyrd had to return home to collect the harvest. This meant Harold didn't have all of his forces when William invaded, which weakened the Anglo-Saxons.
   - Luck was an important factor in William's victory at the Battle of Hastings. Harold had been prepared for a Norman invasion throughout mid-1066. However, the Normans had to delay crossing the Channel due to poor weather conditions, so they didn't arrive when Harold expected them to. Instead, William arrived a couple of days after Harold's army had fought at the Battle of Stamford Bridge, giving the Normans an advantage.

William I in Power: Securing the Kingdom, 1066-1087

Page 21 — William Becomes King of England

Knowledge and Understanding

1
   - 14th October 1066 — Harold Godwinson is killed and William wins the Battle of Hastings.
   - October-November 1066 — Earl Edwin of Mercia, Earl Morcar of Northumbria and other powerful Anglo-Saxon nobles claim Edgar Atheling is their rightful king and take refuge in London. William seizes control of south-eastern England to prepare an attack on London, and the Anglo-Saxons aren't able to gather a large enough army to fight against him.
   - Early-Mid December 1066 — The submission of the earls. Edwin, Morcar, Edgar and other Anglo-Saxon nobles meet with William and surrender to him.
   - 25th December 1066 — William is crowned King of England at Westminster Abbey.

2 a) The Scottish gave refuge to fleeing Anglo-Saxons and supported their efforts to oppose the Normans.
  b) Harold Godwinson's sons were in exile in Ireland and made attacks against the Normans in England.
  c) The Danish kings felt they still had a claim to the English throne, so they could potentially attack England.

Thinking Historically

1 a) This meant the most powerful Anglo-Saxon nobles had promised loyalty to William, which reduced the risk of rebellion. It also ended Edgar Atheling's claim to the throne, paving the way for William to become king.
  b) This encouraged Anglo-Saxon nobles to accept William's rule because they would be allowed to keep their land if they did. It also showed that William was aiming to keep aspects of Edward's rule the same, which encouraged people to see him as Edward's true successor.

Answers

c) This rewarded William's followers for their support in the conquest and encouraged them to remain loyal to him. It also ensured he had loyal fighters in England when he needed them.

d) This helped to prevent invasions from Wales and to stop the Welsh providing support or refuge to Anglo-Saxon rebels. The Marcher earldoms were controlled by some of William's closest allies, which meant he could rely on them to keep the area under control.

Page 23 — Norman Castles

Knowledge and Understanding

1 a) These castles were built when William first invaded England. They gave him a strong base from which he could fight for the English throne.
  b) They were built on the south coast to protect England from an invasion by sea.
  c) They were built in the Marcher earldoms to defend England against potential attacks from Wales.
  d) It was built after the Normans defeated a rebellion in Exeter in 1068.

2 According to Domesday Book, there were 50 castles in England by 1086, and all but one of these had been built between 1066 and 1086.

3 The Anglo-Saxons didn't have much experience of fighting against enemies in castles, which made it harder for them to overcome the Normans' defences. They also didn't have many strong fortifications they could use to defend against the Normans' attacks.

Thinking Historically

1 a) By using castles to control important towns, roads and rivers, the Normans ensured that they weren't cut off from each other. This strengthened the Norman army. It also made it more difficult for Anglo-Saxon rebels to move around the country, which weakened the Anglo-Saxon resistance.
  b) This meant that William could station Norman troops all across England. This allowed the Normans to respond quickly to unrest wherever it broke out.
  c) Having a strong base helped the Normans to attack more successfully, which made it easier for them to take control of more land across England.

2 Castles were built in order to put down Anglo-Saxon resistance and secure the Normans' invasion of England. This meant that castles symbolised the use of violence against the Anglo-Saxons. Some castles were built on the sites of Anglo-Saxon thegns' residences as a symbol that the Normans had replaced the Anglo-Saxons as rulers of England. The large number of castles that the Normans built symbolised their dominance and military strength.

Page 25 — The Design of Norman Castles

Knowledge and Understanding

1 a) The motte was a cone-shaped mound of earth with a flat top, normally built next to a bailey but sometimes built inside it. Mottes ranged from 3m to 30m in height and were usually manmade.
  b) The bailey was an enclosed space surrounded by high walls. It was usually on one side of the motte and built on raised earthworks. The bailey contained most of the castle's living accommodation, which could include housing, stables and a chapel.
  c) The keep, sometimes known as a tower, was a structure built at the top of the motte.

2 Wooden castles could be built quickly and without skilled labour. When the Normans first arrived in England, it was important for them to build castles quickly to help them establish control in England.

3 a) Richmond Castle was built next to a steep drop into the River Swale.
  b) Exeter Castle was just a fortified enclosure and didn't have a motte or a keep.
  c) Pevensey Castle was built inside an Anglo-Saxon fortification that had existed before the conquest.

Thinking Historically

1 a) The ditch surrounded the motte and bailey and could be filled with water to create a moat, making it difficult for attackers to reach the motte and bailey. Ditches sometimes separated the motte and bailey, meaning the motte could be defended even if the bailey was captured.
  b) The raised earthworks were used as a base to build the motte and bailey on. This created a high bank, which made the castle easier to defend.
  c) The palisade was a fence of sharpened wooden stakes. Palisades were often built around the motte and the bailey to make it more difficult for attackers to climb over the wall and get inside.
  d) The bridge was the only way of crossing the ditch to reach the bailey. At the end of the bridge was a gatehouse where guards could be stationed. This made it difficult for attackers to enter the bailey and helped to protect the motte, which could only be reached by going through the bailey.

Page 27 — Resistance to Norman Rule, 1068-1069

Knowledge and Understanding

1 Mercia, 1068:
  - Edwin of Mercia
  - Morcar of Northumbria
  - Bleddyn, a Welsh lord

Answers

Northumbria, 1069:
- Edgar Atheling
- King Malcolm III of Scotland
- King Swein II of Denmark
- Northern nobles

2 a) William hurries north and puts down the rebellion. He also builds a second castle at York and strengthens the Norman forces in Northumbria.
b) The Danes help the remaining northern rebels take York, capturing both Norman castles there and taking control of Northumbria.
c) William is able to scatter the Anglo-Saxon rebels, who no longer have the support of the Danes. He regains control of Northumbria.

Thinking Historically

1 They show how difficult it was for William to find a balance of power that kept the Anglo-Saxon nobles happy. William allowed Anglo-Saxon lords to remain in power if they supported him, but he couldn't give them too much power otherwise they could become a threat to his rule. This led to resentment among earls like Edwin and Morcar, who rebelled in order to try and gain more power.

2 The rebellions were separate rather than being a united movement of resistance against the Normans. For example, the rebels weren't led by a single leader, they were motivated by local concerns rather than common goals, and they didn't coordinate their rebellions with a shared strategy. The rebels also weren't supported by all Anglo-Saxons — many nobles supported William and fought for him, while others didn't take sides. All of these factors weakened the Anglo-Saxons' attempts to resist the Normans.

3 You can choose any reason, as long as you explain your answer. For example:
The main reason the northern revolt in 1069 failed was because the rebels weren't a unified force. This lack of unity helped William put an end to the revolt. He came to an agreement with the Danes, who agreed to return to their ships, allowing William to scatter the remaining Anglo-Saxon rebels. If the Anglo-Saxons and the Danes had remained united, it would have been more difficult for William to end the revolt.

Page 29 — The Harrying of the North

Knowledge and Understanding

1 The Harrying of the North was William's response to the 1069 rebellion, where he laid waste to large parts of northern England.

2 The northern revolt in 1069 had been a serious threat to William, and there were also other rebellions taking place all over the country. William's aim with the Harrying was to prevent future rebellions in the north by destroying the northern rebels' supplies and support. He also wanted to deter other rebellions by sending a message to the rest of the country about what to expect if they rebelled.

Thinking Historically

1 William had taken a lenient approach to rebels in previous revolts. For example, he allowed Edwin and Morcar to keep their lives and freedom after their rebellion in Mercia in 1068. In contrast, his reaction to the northern revolt in 1069 was harsh and brutal, as he punished everyone in the region and not just the leaders of the revolt.

2
- Many villages were burned and destroyed.
- Many people starved because the Normans destroyed food and livestock.
- Many northerners became refugees and fled to other parts of England or to Scotland.
- Many people who stayed in the north after the Harrying faced disease.
- Northerners joined other rebellions, such as the one led by Hereward the Wake in East Anglia.
- The economy of the north was damaged.

3 a) Evidence for — The Harrying shows that the Normans used cruel methods to oppress the Anglo-Saxons, such as slaughtering people and destroying villages.
Evidence against — The Normans' tactic of laying waste to enemy territory wasn't uncommon in the 11th century, so William's actions weren't necessarily cruel by the moral standards of the time.
b) Evidence for — Domesday Book describes many northern villages in 1086 as 'waste', suggesting that the Harrying caused long-term damage to the northern economy.
Evidence against — Villages and towns were described as 'waste' in Domesday Book for a number of reasons, e.g. because they didn't pay their taxes. This means that the term 'waste' doesn't necessarily reflect the impact of the Harrying. This means the information in Domesday Book isn't that useful for analysing the damage caused by the Harrying.

Answers

4   You can answer either way, as long as you explain your answer. For example:
    - William could have maintained control of England without the Harrying of the North. William had successfully put down every Anglo-Saxon rebellion against him, showing he was capable of maintaining control of England without resorting to such cruel tactics. For example, he ended Edwin and Morcar's rebellion in 1068 by building a castle and proving his military strength, which caused them to surrender. This shows that there were other methods William could have used to maintain control of England instead of the Harrying of the North.
    - William could not have maintained control of England without the Harrying of the North. He had tried peaceful methods of preventing rebellions such as allowing Anglo-Saxon nobles to keep their land if they accepted his rule. Despite this, there were still many Anglo-Saxon rebellions. Therefore, William needed to find a more effective way of maintaining control and deterring future rebellions. The Harrying achieved this because it sent a powerful message to the rest of the country about what to expect if they rebelled. Another reason why William could not have maintained control without the Harrying is that the 1069 revolt posed a serious threat to him because the rebels were a large force made up of the Anglo-Saxons, the Scottish and the Danes. While dealing with this, William was also facing other rebellions elsewhere in the country. This serious threat meant William had little choice but to carry out the Harrying in order to maintain control of the country by forcing the northern rebels to submit.

Page 31 — Resistance to Norman Rule, 1070-1071

Knowledge and Understanding

1   a) William pays the Danes to abandon Hereward.
    b) Hereward and Morcar take control of the Isle of Ely and try to hold it against William's army.
    c) Hereward survives the attack on Ely, but his whereabouts and actions after the rebellion in East Anglia are unknown.
2   Before the rebellions, William tried to work with the Anglo-Saxon nobles. After the rebellions between 1068 and 1071, he no longer felt he had to keep the Anglo-Saxons happy.
3   Normanisation was the process of making England 'more Norman', for example by replacing powerful Anglo-Saxons in the government and in the Church with Normans.

4
    - William took away land belonging to the Anglo-Saxons and gave it to loyal Normans.
    - William changed the size of English estates. He turned larger areas of land into smaller estates.
    - William reorganised estates so that a lord's lands were all in the same region. Before the conquest, some Anglo-Saxon lords had owned areas of land in different parts of the country.
    - William increased the amount of land in England held by the king.
    - William limited the amount of land each noble family could hold.

Thinking Historically

1   Making estates smaller and more compact meant they were easier to defend against military threats. By making the estates smaller and limiting the amount of land each noble family could hold, William reduced the power of these families and ensured they didn't have enough strength to threaten him as king. William also increased his power by increasing the proportion of lands held by the king. This put him in a stronger position than the nobles and made them less likely to challenge him.
2   a) This increased William's personal control of the government.
    b) William replaced Anglo-Saxons in government with loyal Normans. This strengthened William's control by ensuring he could rely on the people in his government, as the Normans he appointed were less likely to rebel against him than the Anglo-Saxons had been.
    c) Castles were built across the whole kingdom and were used as centres of local government. This strengthened William's control as it meant local government officials dealt with responsibilities in their lands such as collecting taxes and enforcing law and order.

Page 33 — The Revolt of the Earls

Knowledge and Understanding

1   They felt they had less power and influence than their fathers had done and they resented William for restricting their power.
2   a) Roger made an alliance with Ralph de Gael, and then joined forces with Earl Waltheof. During the revolt, he barely made it out of Hereford before being captured.
    b) Ralph made an alliance with Roger de Breteuil and married Emma, Roger's sister. He also made an alliance with Earl Waltheof. During the revolt, he escaped the siege of Norwich Castle and went to Denmark for reinforcements.
    c) Emma was left in control of Norwich Castle during its long siege, but eventually surrendered to the Norman forces.

Answers

d) Waltheof joined forces with Ralph de Gael and Roger de Breteuil. He later betrayed the rebels by confessing the plans of the revolt to King William.

e) Lanfranc was acting as regent in England at the time of the revolt. After William told him about Waltheof's confession, he reacted swiftly, sending troops to Roger and Ralph's earldoms and ending the revolt.

f) The Danes came to England to support the revolt after Ralph de Gael asked for their assistance. However, the Danish reinforcements arrived too late to provide support to the rebels.

3 William was in Normandy.

4 Earl Waltheof was treated more harshly than Roger and Ralph. Waltheof was the only one who was executed for his part in the rebellion. Roger was imprisoned for life and Ralph gave up his lands and went into exile.

Thinking Historically

1 Here are some points your answer may include:
- The only Anglo-Saxon earl involved in the revolt was beheaded, while the foreign earls were treated more leniently. This may have suggested that there were more serious consequences for Anglo-Saxons who rebelled, making them more reluctant to revolt.
- There had been many Anglo-Saxon rebellions between 1067 and 1075, but none of them had succeeded in overthrowing Norman rule. The Anglo-Saxons might have been so demoralised by these repeated failures that they no longer had the will to rebel.
- This was the first major revolt to involve foreign earls, who were far more powerful that the Anglo-Saxons. However, even with their power the revolt was unsuccessful. This may have suggested that William was too powerful to resist and made the Anglo-Saxons feel there was no way they could overthrow the Normans.

2 Northern Revolt, 1069:
- The Anglo-Saxon rebels were supported by the Scots and the Danes, who were powerful allies.
- The rebels managed to take control of Northumbria, a large area of England.
- There were other rebellions going on at the same time, such as Eadric the Wild's rebellion in Shrewsbury.

The Revolt of the Earls, 1075:
- The revolt was started by earls from Normandy and Brittany who were expected to be loyal to William.
- The earls involved held a lot of land across England, which gave them wealth and power.
- The earls had support from the Danish.
- William wasn't in the country at the time of the revolt so he couldn't personally help to put the revolt down.

3 You can answer either way, as long as you explain your answer. For example:
- The northern revolt in 1069 posed more of a threat to William's rule than the Revolt of the Earls. The rebels involved in the northern revolt managed to take control of Northumbria, a large and important area of England. On the other hand, the Revolt of the Earls was stopped before either Ralph or Roger got out of their earldoms. This meant they weren't able to take any land from William and posed less of a threat than those who took part in the northern revolt in 1069.
- The Revolt of the Earls in 1075 posed more of a threat to William's rule. Most of the revolts against William were led by Anglo-Saxons, but the 1075 revolt was led by earls from Normandy and Brittany. These earls were expected to be loyal to William, but their revolt showed that some of William's own supporters were dissatisfied with how he was running the kingdom. The Norman nobility were key to William's control of the country, and if more of them had joined the revolt it could have been difficult to put down, making it a larger threat than the northern revolt in 1069.

Page 35 — Exam-Style Questions

1 Each aspect is marked separately and you can have a maximum of two marks per aspect. How to grade your answer:
- 1 mark for describing one credible aspect of the Marcher earldoms.
- 2 marks for describing one credible aspect of the Marcher earldoms and using your own knowledge to back it up.

Here are some points your answer may include:
- The Marcher earldoms were built along the border between England and Wales. This border was an unstable area.
- The Marcher earldoms were given to Norman earls like Roger of Montgomery and William FitzOsbern, who were some of William's closest allies.
- The Marcher earldoms were created so William could control the Welsh Marches. William didn't have the military power or money to control this area himself.

2 This question is level marked. You should look at the level descriptions on page 59 to help you mark your answer.

Here are some points your answer may include:
- The Revolt of the Earls failed because William had installed a trusted supporter, Archbishop Lanfranc, as regent. Lanfranc was a capable regent who was able to quickly put an end to the revolt.

Answers

- The revolt failed because Earl Waltheof, who was one of the rebels, betrayed Roger de Breteuil and Ralph de Gael by confessing their plan to King William. Waltheof's warning meant that William and Lanfranc were prepared for a rebellion against them, which gave them an advantage over the rebels.
- William and Lanfranc reacted quickly to the information they were given and this contributed to the failure of the revolt. Their quick response allowed them to trap Roger and Ralph in their earldoms, which limited the impact of the revolt.
- There wasn't enough Anglo-Saxon support for the revolt. The Anglo-Saxons were reluctant to risk themselves to try and increase the power of Roger de Breteuil and Ralph de Gael, two foreign lords. This lack of support made it easier to put an end to the revolt.
- Danish reinforcements didn't arrive in time to support the revolt. The Danes had provided important support to rebellions in the past, such as the revolt in northern England in 1069 when a Danish fleet helped rebels seize Northumbria. The lack of Danish reinforcements in 1075 contributed to the failure of the Revolt of the Earls.

3 This question is level marked. You should look at the level descriptions on page 59 to help you mark your answer.
Here are some points your answer may include:

- The Anglo-Saxon rebellions failed to overthrow William's rule because they were individual uprisings rather than a collective national movement. This meant the Anglo-Saxon attacks weren't coordinated and William was able to send local forces to deal with smaller rebellions, such as Eadric the Wild's attack on Shrewsbury, while he dealt with larger threats, such as the revolt in northern England. This made it easier for William to put down these rebellions and was a significant reason why William stayed in power.
- William stayed in power because the Anglo-Saxon nobility was divided between those who supported William and those who supported the Anglo-Saxon rebels. Many of the nobles supported William by helping him fight the rebels, while others didn't get involved in the fighting at all. This weakened the threat of the Anglo-Saxon rebellions, meaning they didn't have the strength to overthrow William.
- An important reason William was able to stay in power was his success in breaking up the weak alliances between the Anglo-Saxon rebels and their foreign allies. For example, William was able to reach an agreement with the Danes during the northern revolt in 1069, causing the Danes to return to their ships. This left the Anglo-Saxon rebels unsupported and led to the failure of the rebellion. William's exploitation of this weak alliance helped him to stay in power.
- William built many castles after the conquest, and the multiple strengths of castles meant they were an important reason why he remained in power. Castles were strong bases from which the Normans could launch attacks and defend against Anglo-Saxon violence. The network of castles throughout England allowed William to quickly put down resistance wherever it broke out. William also used castles to take hold of strategically important places such as roads and rivers, which stopped Anglo-Saxon rebels moving around the country freely.
- One of the most important ways William established and maintained control was through Normanisation (making England 'more Norman'). William achieved this by seizing land from Anglo-Saxon nobles and giving it to loyal Normans. He also replaced Anglo-Saxons in the government and the Church with his Norman supporters. This strengthened William's power in England by ensuring he could trust and rely on the most powerful people in the country.
- William stayed in power because of his use of violence against Anglo-Saxon rebels. After the northern revolt in 1069, William ordered the Harrying of the North to destroy supplies and sources of support for northern rebels, and to send a severe warning to any other Anglo-Saxons who might try to rebel. This prevented further rebellions in the north and meant he faced fewer challenges to his power.
- William's control of the Welsh border helped him to stay in power. He created the Marcher earldoms and gave them to his most trusted supporters. This made it more difficult for the Welsh to provide support or refuge to Anglo-Saxon rebels, which helped William stay in power by making it harder for the Anglo-Saxons to rebel against him.

Norman England, 1066-1088

Page 37 — Norman Society

Knowledge and Understanding

1
- King — He was the wealthiest and most powerful person in society. He owned all of the land in England. He gave land to his subjects but could take it away if he chose.
- Tenants-in-chief — They held land directly from the king. They included archbishops, bishops, earls and barons.

Answers

- Knights — They were similar to thegns in Anglo-Saxon society, although the main service they provided to their lord was military. They were given land by their lord.
- Peasants — Their lives were very similar to how they had been in Anglo-Saxon England. They farmed the land. The number of slaves decreased in Norman England.

2 The feudal system was based on vassalic bonds, which meant lords gave land to their vassals in return for their loyalty. Vassals would pay homage to their lord (the king or one of his tenants-in-chief) by kneeling before him and swearing an oath of loyalty, and in return the lord would swear to protect the vassal. If a vassal broke the agreement with their lord, then they could be forced to give up their land. This was known as forfeiture. This threat of losing land encouraged vassals to be loyal to their lords.

Thinking Historically

1 a) Change — In Anglo-Saxon England, the king allowed his earls to own large areas of land. In Norman England, the king owned all of the land and his tenants-in-chief only held their land with his permission.
   b) Continuity — Lords still gave out land and offered protection to dependents in return for service.
   c) Continuity — The role of a peasant didn't change much. They still farmed land for their lord as they had done in Anglo-Saxon England.
   d) Change — The number of slaves decreased after the conquest.

2 In Norman society, the king owned all of the land, meaning he was very powerful. The Norman earls held land with the king's permission, but as the king owned it he was able to take it away again. This meant the king had a lot of power over his earls. In Anglo-Saxon England, earls owned their own land so they had more power than Norman earls. This meant the Anglo-Saxon king relied on the support of his earls to rule the kingdom more than the king did in Norman England.

Page 39 — Norman Government

Knowledge and Understanding

1
- The majority of the population in both periods was made up of Anglo-Saxons.
- Peasants made up the vast majority of the population in both periods.

2 In a centralised government, power is focused around one figure, e.g. in Norman England power was focused around the king.

3 The lands held by William's 'inner circle' were smaller than the earldoms that had belonged to earls in Anglo-Saxon England.

4 William used regents to rule England when he was out of the country fulfilling his duties as Duke of Normandy. William gave the regents the same authority as the king so they could govern England effectively. He chose trusted supporters to be regents, such as Odo of Bayeux and Archbishop Lanfranc.

Thinking Historically

1 The rebellions showed that William's policy of trying to work with the Anglo-Saxons wasn't working and they would continue to be a threat if he left them in power. Replacing the Anglo-Saxon nobles with Normans reduced this threat by reducing the Anglo-Saxons' power and making it harder for them to rebel.

2 a) William increased the use of writs compared to Anglo-Saxon England. Writs allowed William to send royal commands via documents to local government officials. This enabled William to take a direct role in governing the country, which increased his power.
   b) William gave sheriffs more responsibilty in local government. This meant he had strong, loyal supporters all over England to carry out his commands, giving him more control over local government.
   c) William reduced the power of earls by giving them smaller earldoms. As earls were the most powerful people in the kingdom after the king, this increased the gap in power between William and others in the kingdom.

Page 41 — Norman Government

Knowledge and Understanding

1 He didn't want them to become powerful enough to rebel against him.

2 The royal demesne was the land that the king kept for himself rather than giving to vassals. This made up around one quarter of all the land in England.

3 William wanted to create continuity with King Edward's reign to show that he was Edward's true successor. Keeping laws that had existed during Edward's reign was one way of doing this.

4 a) This new law set aside large areas of the country as royal forest for William to hunt in. Ordinary people weren't allowed to use the royal forest and were severely punished if they did.
   b) The murdrum fine was introduced to prevent Norman settlers being attacked or killed by Anglo-Saxons. If a Norman was murdered and the killer wasn't caught, the whole village where the Norman was murdered would have to pay a large fine.

Answers

5. It stopped ordinary people from hunting or gathering food in the royal forest, which limited the areas where they could get food. It also resulted in some villages being destroyed to clear land for hunting, meaning some ordinary people lost their homes.

Thinking Historically

1. Change:
   - Sheriffs were given more power.
   - They were able to perform their duties with less interference from earls.
   - Sheriffs became responsible for the royal demesne.
   - Sheriffs were wealthier than they had been in Anglo-Saxon England.

   Continuity:
   - They collected fines and taxes at a local level.
   - They oversaw criminal cases at local courts.
   - They organised and often led military forces.
   - Sheriffs were appointed by the king.

2. a) William's decision to increase the power of sheriffs reduced the power of earls. The increase in the power of the sheriffs meant earls had less influence over how their lands were managed. This made it harder for them to challenge William and allowed him to maintain control over them.
   b) William's changes to the power of sheriffs caused problems for him and made it more difficult to maintain control of earls. Increasing the power of sheriffs reduced the influence of earls, which led to resentment from the earls. Some earls were so resentful about their lack of power that they launched a rebellion against William in 1075, which is known as the Revolt of the Earls. This suggests that increasing the power of the sheriffs made it harder for William to maintain control over earls.
   c) Overall, William's changes to the power of sheriffs did help him maintain control over earls. The sheriffs took over important duties belonging to the earls which reduced the power and influence of earls. Although this caused resentment among the earls, not all earls rebelled during the Revolt of the Earls in 1075. This suggests William had control over most of the earls.

Page 43 — Life in Norman England

Knowledge and Understanding

1. a)
   - Soldiers lived in castles and they increased the demand for goods and services.
   - Towns often developed around newly built castles, creating new centres of economic activity.
   - Markets were sometimes set up inside castles because they provided a safe place to trade.

   b)
   - Craftsmen were needed to help build the churches. This created employment, which helped the economy grow.

   c)
   - Trade encouraged people to come to England from abroad, including merchants and traders. This increase in population and business helped towns to recover, which contributed to economic growth.
   - Trade grew between England and parts of France, including Normandy. England exported goods such as wool to other countries, and this increase in business boosted the economy.

Thinking Historically

1.
   - Towns such as Nottingham grew in size, while new towns such as St Albans also developed.
   - More people started to live in towns — some people in England moved from villages to towns and people from abroad also settled in English towns.
   - Towns became centres of trade and administration. They also had military and religious functions because castles and churches were built in towns. This meant that towns served a more important role in Norman England than they had in Anglo-Saxon England.

2. a) Evidence for — Peasants still lived in villages and worked on farms.
   Evidence against — The number of slaves began to decline at a greater pace after the conquest.
   b) Evidence for — New markets were set up in English towns and there was an increase in international trade.
   Evidence against — The north of England didn't benefit from economic growth. The gap in wealth between the north and the south increased between 1066 and 1086.
   c) Evidence for — Castles contributed to the growth of towns. They housed soldiers, which created a demand for goods and services and helped the economy to grow.
   Evidence against — Buildings were torn down in some towns to make way for castles.

3. You can choose how far you agree with each statement, as long as you explain your answer. For example:
   a) I agree that the conquest didn't affect people very much at the lowest levels of society. The majority of peasants who lived in villages remained there after the conquest and continued to do farm work. The reduction in slavery was already happening before the conquest, meaning the Normans just continued a process that had already started. As a result, the conquest didn't really affect people at this level of society.

Answers

b) I disagree that the conquest had a positive impact on England's economy. Although the economy grew in parts of the country, it didn't grow in the north. Towns in southern England, such as Canterbury, became wealthier, but towns in the north had been damaged by the Harrying of the North and struggled to recover. This means that the economy of a large area of England wasn't positively affected by the conquest.

c) I agree that castles were beneficial for English towns. Castles could cause some damage to towns because buildings were destroyed to make way for castles. However, castles also housed soldiers, who required goods and services in the town, and provided secure places to trade. These factors helped towns to recover and encouraged growth. Therefore, castles were beneficial for English towns in the long term.

Page 45 — Domesday Book

Knowledge and Understanding

1. Domesday Book is a survey and valuation of all the land and resources in England, carried out in 1086. It contains records of the land held by the king, his tenants-in-chief and their vassals, as well as who held the land in 1066 and how much the land was worth in 1086.
2. England was divided into shires and hundreds and governed locally, which made it possible to collect information for Domesday Book. The Anglo-Saxon taxation records also provided information that was useful for Domesday Book.
3. It gives detailed information from before and after the conquest. This helps historians study how England changed over time and lets them judge the impact that the conquest had on England.
4. a) Tenants-in-chief, alongside government officials in each shire, made lists of who owned the land and gave these to commissioners.
   b) Commissioners compared lists of who owned the land with existing records about land ownership. They also asked juries about the ownership and value of land.
   c) Juries were summoned from each hundred to special meetings of the shire courts to provide information about the ownership and value of land. They were made up of equal numbers of Anglo-Saxons and Normans to ensure that the information was accurate from before and after the conquest.

Thinking Historically

1. a) Domesday Book told the king how much land was worth and therefore he knew how much tax should be paid for that land. It also helped him to see when someone had inherited land so he could demand additional tax.
   b) Domesday Book created a detailed written record of who owned what, which could be used to settle the dispute.
   c) Domesday Book provided information such as how many knights the king could summon to fight for him.

Page 47 — Norman Culture

Knowledge and Understanding

1. Trial by combat was a way of trying someone for a crime. A person accused of a crime could challenge their accuser to a fight to the death instead of being tried in court. The Normans believed that God would help whoever was innocent to win the fight. Trial by combat was a new custom the Normans brought over to England.
2. The Normans brought England up to date with architectural fashions in Western Europe by popularising the Romanesque style of architecture in England. This type of architecture used features inspired by Roman buildings, such as high arches and wide columns.
3. They believed that supporting the Church was a way of serving God.
4.
   - The Normans gave the Church gifts of land, which was used to build more churches.
   - The Normans rebuilt many parish churches and many of the major churches in England.
   - They founded new monasteries, such as Shrewsbury Abbey, which was founded in 1083.

Thinking Historically

1. a) Before the conquest, people in England spoke Old English. After the conquest, Old English changed to include French words.
   b) Norman settlers in England spoke Old French and introduced French loanwords into English.
   c) Before the conquest, the main written language was Old English. After the conquest, Latin became the dominant language for written texts.
   d) William introduced bilingual documents that were written in both Old English and Latin so they could be understood by Anglo-Saxons and Normans. However, he issued governments documents almost exclusively in Latin after 1070.
2. You can answer either way, as long as you explain your answer. For example:
   - The Norman Conquest had a significant effect on culture in England because it led to changes in lots of different areas. For example, the Normans influenced food and clothing, introduced new customs such as trial by combat, and changed the language used in government documents from Old English to Latin. This shows that the Norman Conquest had a widespread and significant impact on culture in England.

Answers

- The Norman Conquest did not have a significant effect on culture in England because cultural changes only impacted the nobility, who represented a minority of the population. Cultural changes didn't really affect people lower down in the social hierarchy, such as peasants, who made up the majority of the population in Norman England.

Page 49 — The Norman Church

Knowledge and Understanding

1. a) Senior Anglo-Saxon churchmen were replaced with Normans — by 1087, there was only one Anglo-Saxon bishop in England.
   b) There wasn't much change for ordinary churchmen — there were still a lot of Anglo-Saxon monks and the majority of parish priests were Anglo-Saxon in 1087.
2. a) Pluralism was the act of a churchman holding more than one religious office at the same time.
   b) Simony was the act of buying or selling positions in the Church.
   c) Nepotism was the act of giving positions in the Church to friends or family members.
   d) Clerical marriage was when churchmen had wives or mistresses, despite the fact they were meant to remain unmarried.
3.
   - They restructured the Church to make it more centralised, so that the Archbishop of Canterbury had more power and influence.
   - They used councils to impose discipline on churchmen.
   - They introduced church courts to try churchmen who broke religious laws.
4. The Normans brought new churchmen to England who were keen on reform, which might have made the process of reform happen more quickly.

Thinking Historically

1. a) Lanfranc — He was a supporter of Church reform and wanted to get rid of corrupt practices, such as simony and nepotism. On the other hand, Stigand committed pluralism by being Bishop of Winchester at the same time as he was Archbishop of Canterbury, suggesting he wasn't against these corrupt practices.
   b) Both — Stigand was useful as he was a powerful Anglo-Saxon and he was able to negotiate with the Anglo-Saxons on William's behalf. Lanfranc was useful because he was a supporter of William. When he became Archbishop, it meant that the most powerful member of the Church was no longer an Anglo-Saxon, which increased William's control over England.
   c) Stigand — In 1070, William allowed the Pope's representatives to remove Stigand as Archbishop of Canterbury for pluralism.
2. Stigand had supported many of William's Anglo-Saxon rivals — he had been an ally of Harold Godwinson, and had backed Edwin and Morcar when they tried to overthrow William and put Edgar Atheling on the throne. This suggested Stigand's loyalties were with the Anglo-Saxons, whereas Lanfranc was a foreign supporter who backed William as king, making him a more trustworthy ally.
3. The Church was a powerful institution in Norman England. It held large areas of land, played a role in the government and was able to influence ordinary people's opinions. Therefore, being in control of the Church gave the king a lot of power and influence which helped him to control the kingdom.

Page 51 — Bishop Odo of Bayeux

Knowledge and Understanding

1.
   - 1049 — Odo is made Bishop of Bayeux by his half-brother, William.
   - 1066 — Odo supports William's claim to the English throne by providing him with men and ships for his invasion. He also fights alongside William at the Battle of Hastings. In return for his support, William makes Odo Earl of Kent.
   - 1067 — Odo is named as a regent when William returns to Normandy. In the same year, the people of Kent rebel against Odo, working with a foreign lord called Eustace of Boulogne to try to take Dover Castle.
   - 1070s — Odo is accused of taking land that belongs to the Church and is tried in court. He is ordered to return some of the lands he obtained.
   - 1082 — Odo gathers troops to take to Italy, possibly to try and make himself the Pope. He is arrested and imprisoned by William.
2. Odo was responsible for maintaining control of the south east of England, an important area that was used by the Normans for crossing between England and Normandy. He was also responsible for governing the lands in his earldom and maintaining control of the people who lived there.
3. Odo was unpopular because he seized lands and wealth from nobles in his earldom. This led the people of Kent to rebel against him.

Answers

Thinking Historically

1. Odo played a key role in Norman England over a long period of time. Odo provided support for William during the Battle of Hastings, including men and ships. This helped William defeat Harold Godwinson, removing his main rival for the throne of England. Odo also helped William secure his rule of England by maintaining firm control over south east England, which ensured that the Normans could travel between England and Normandy. He also used harsh measures against the Anglo-Saxons in Kent which helped secure Norman rule. However, he later came into conflict with Archbishop Lanfranc, who accused Odo of stealing land from the Church. This shows that while Odo was important in helping William gain and secure the throne, he was also a controversial figure who caused trouble for William.

2. Odo's reign shows that the earls relied on William for their power and that their power was only secure if William favoured them. For example, William realised that Odo was a strong supporter of his in 1066, and so made him Earl of Kent as he knew he could rely on him. However, once Odo became too ambitious and wanted more power, gathering an army to take to Italy, William arrested him and stripped him of his earldom. This shows that earls could lose their power if they displeased William or if it seemed that they might become a threat to him.

3. a) This created conflict with Archbishop Lanfranc, the most powerful man in the English Church. Lanfranc and the Church had a lot of influence in England, and Odo was forced to give up some of the land he had taken. This loss of land reduced his power.
   b) It suggested Odo was gaining too much power and could potentially prove to be a military threat to William. This led to William arresting and imprisoning Odo.
   c) Odo treated the people in his earldom harshly and took lands and wealth from them. This made him unpopular with the people in Kent and led to rebellions against his rule, which may have caused William to remove him as earl.

Page 53 — William I and Robert Curthose

Knowledge and Understanding

1. The different sources create contradictory accounts of what William was like. Most of the Norman sources were written by William's supporters, who wanted to present him in a positive way. However, Anglo-Saxon sources were written by people who saw William as an invader.

2. Robert wanted more responsibility and authority, but William refused to give this to him. This caused Robert to resent his father. When Robert asked to rule Normandy while William ruled England, William wouldn't allow it and Robert rebelled against him.

3. a) Robert raids the surrounding area and forces William to meet him in battle.
   b) Many people, including Norman lords and William's wife Matilda, encourage William to reconcile with Robert.
   c) Robert goes back into exile, where he remains until William's death.

4. It was a humiliating defeat for William and it showed him that Robert was a serious threat.

Thinking Historically

1. Here are some points your answer may include:
   - Point — William used extreme violence against the Anglo-Saxons.
   - Evidence — He ordered the Harrying of the North, which involved slaughtering people and destroying their villages and food supplies.
   - Why evidence supports point — The Harrying took place as a response to a rebellion, but it's likely innocent people ended up suffering as well as the rebels. It was so harsh that it caused a lot of damage to the north, creating a famine and causing many people to die of disease or starvation. The widespread death and destruction in the north show that William was cruel towards his Anglo-Saxon subjects.
   - Point — William wasn't a cruel king because he was generous to his loyal followers.
   - Evidence — William gave land and titles to his Norman supporters. For example, he named his half-brother, Odo, Earl of Kent for supporting him at the Battle of Hastings, making Odo very powerful and wealthy.
   - Why evidence supports point — As a result of William's generosity, many of his followers prospered in England. This shows that he was willing to reward those who he felt were deserving and suggests William wasn't cruel to those who supported his reign as king.
   - Point — William's actions were practical rather than cruel.
   - Evidence — William tried to work with the Anglo-Saxon nobles, and only removed them from positions of power after they kept rebelling against him.
   - Why evidence supports point — William used harsh measures only as a last resort. His efforts to work with the Anglo-Saxons failed, and he needed to act to prevent further threats to his rule. Therefore, he removed Anglo-Saxons from power to maintain control and stabilise England, not necessarily because he was cruel and wanted to cause suffering for the Anglo-Saxons.

Answers

Page 55 — The Death of William I

Knowledge and Understanding

1
- Robert Curthose, William's eldest son, became Duke of Normandy.
- William Rufus, William's second son, became King of England.
- Henry, William's youngest son, was given £5000.

2 To secure his position as King of England, William Rufus sailed for England a couple of days before William I died. William Rufus met with Archbishop Lanfranc when he arrived. It was important to gain Lanfranc's support as Lanfranc had a lot of influence in England and had the power to crown the new king. By getting Lanfranc's support quickly, William Rufus was able to secure his claim to the English throne.

3
- 9th Sept 1087 — William I dies.
- 26th Sept 1087 — William II is crowned King of England by Lanfranc in Westminster Abbey.
- 1088 — Odo of Bayeux leads a rebellion against William II, believing that Robert Curthose should be King of England. However the rebellion fails and Odo is sent into exile by William II.
- 1096 — Robert gives Normandy to William II, meaning William controls both Normandy and England.
- 1100 — William II is killed in a hunting accident. Henry, William I's youngest son, becomes King of England.

4 Odo planned to gain support from enough lords that he could overthrow William II. He also planned to gain control of the south coast of England to secure a passage for reinforcements from Normandy.

5 Odo was unable to get enough support for the rebellion because most of the lords remained loyal to William II. Robert and his reinforcements remained in Normandy, leaving Odo unsupported.

Thinking Historically

1 a) Robert might have expected to inherit all of William I's titles and lands, because it was Norman custom for the eldest son to inherit everything. Based on this custom, he felt William Rufus had wrongfully seized the English throne from him.

b) Odo was unhappy with the division of land because he believed that Robert would be easier to control than William Rufus — if Robert was King of England, Odo would be able to increase his own power and influence.

c) Many Norman lords held land in both England and Normandy, meaning they had the difficult task of serving both William II and Robert. To make their lives easier, they wanted just one ruler of England and Normandy. Some Norman lords also felt Robert should have inherited England because he was the eldest son, while others shared Odo's belief that they could gain more power if Robert was King of England.

Page 58 — Exam-Style Questions

1 Each aspect is marked separately and you can have a maximum of two marks per aspect. How to grade your answer:
- 1 mark for describing one credible aspect of the royal forest.
- 2 marks for describing one credible aspect of the royal forest and using your own knowledge to back it up.

Here are some points your answer may include:
- The royal forest was land set aside for the king to hunt in. William established the royal forest by introducing a new law called forest law.
- Ordinary people weren't allowed to use the royal forest. They faced severe punishments if they did use this land.
- The royal forest was unpopular with ordinary people. It limited the areas where they could hunt or gather food.

2 This question is level marked. You should look at the level descriptions on page 59 to help you mark your answer.

Here are some points your answer may include:
- The English Church changed due to William's policy of Normanisation. William replaced senior Anglo-Saxon churchmen with Normans and by 1087 there was only one Anglo-Saxon bishop in England. William made these changes because the Church was a powerful institution in England and he wanted people he could trust in the most important positions within the Church. The introduction of new churchmen contributed to other changes in the Church.
- The appointment of a new Archbishop of Canterbury led to changes in the Church. In 1070, William appointed Lanfranc, a foreign supporter, to replace Stigand, the Anglo-Saxon Archbishop. William did this because he wanted to strengthen his control over England by placing a loyal supporter in the most powerful position in the English Church. Lanfranc's appointment led to change in the Church because Lanfranc wanted to impose stricter rules on the behaviour of churchmen.
- The Church changed because of Lanfranc's efforts to tackle corrupt practices. Before the Norman Conquest, many churchmen in England were corrupt, committing offences such as simony and nepotism. Lanfranc introduced church courts and councils, which helped to tackle these corrupt practices by forcing churchmen to obey religious law.

Answers

- Other foreign churchmen who came to England after the conquest also helped to make the English Church less corrupt. Many of the new churchmen had been influenced by the reform movement in Europe. They brought these ideas to England and encouraged change in the English Church, supporting Lanfranc's efforts at reform.
- The Normans restructured the English Church and made it more centralised in order to give the Archbishop of Canterbury more power. This allowed Lanfranc to assert his authority over churchmen and enforce reforms on the Church.

3 This question is level marked. You should look at the level descriptions on page 59 to help you mark your answer.
   Here are some points your answer may include:
   - The increased power of sheriffs in the government was a significant consequence of the Norman Conquest. William gave sheriffs new responsibilities, such as managing the royal demesne, and ensured they could act with less interference from earls. Sheriffs were sometimes given more land, granting them more wealth, power and status than they had in Anglo-Saxon England.
   - An important consequence of the conquest was the reduced power of earls in the government. William reduced the size of earls' estates and gave some of their responsibilities to sheriffs. As a result, earls were less powerful than they had been in Anglo-Saxon England, meaning it was harder for them to challenge the king, and the king's position was more secure.
   - One of the main consequences of the conquest was that Anglo-Saxons in positions of power were replaced by Normans. After a series of major rebellions against William between 1066-1070, he removed Anglo-Saxons from positions in the government in order to reduce their power. As a result, the Anglo-Saxons had less influence over how the country was run and William strengthened his own control over the kingdom.
   - One important consequence of the conquest was increased centralisation of the government. England was already a centralised kingdom before 1066, but William increased his personal control over the government. For example, he increased the use of writs in order to take a more direct role in running the whole country.
   - One consequence of the conquest was that England was often governed by regents. William was Duke of Normandy as well as King of England, so he spent a lot of time in Normandy, and he appointed regents such as Odo of Bayeux and Archbishop Lanfranc to govern England when he was away. Regents ruled with the same authority as the king, which ensured that England was secure in the king's absence.
   - Another consequence of the Norman Conquest for the government of England was the change to laws regarding hunting and murder. William introduced forest law, which set aside areas of land as royal hunting grounds. He also introduced the murdrum fine, which forced villagers to pay a fine if a Norman was killed and the murderer wasn't found. However, William generally didn't change laws that had existed during King Edward's reign. Therefore, legal changes were only a minor consequence of the conquest because English law was almost the same after 1066 as it had been before.

Index

A

Anglo-Saxon Church 6, 48
archers 16
Atheling, Edgar 12, 20, 26

B

Bayeux Tapestry 10, 50

C

castles 22, 24, 30, 42
cavalry 16
centralisation 30, 38
churches 6, 42, 46
churchmen 4, 6, 48
clerical marriage 48
courts 4, 48
culture 46

D

Domesday Book 22, 28, 38, 42, 44

E

earldoms 4, 38
earls 4, 36, 38, 40
Edward the Confessor, King of England 8, 10, 12, 14
Edwin, Earl of Mercia 14, 20, 26

F

feigned flight 16
feudal system 36
forest law 40
forfeiture 36
fyrd 4, 14, 16

G

Gate Fulford, Battle of 14
Godwin, Earl of Wessex 8
Godwinson, Harold 8, 10, 12, 14, 16
Godwinson, Tostig 8, 10, 12, 14

H

Hardrada, Harald, King of Norway 12, 14
Harrying of the North 28, 42
Hastings, Battle of 16
Hereward the Wake 30
homage 36
housecarls 14, 16
hundreds 4, 38, 44

K

knights 36

L

labour service 4, 36
landownership 4, 20, 30, 36, 38, 44
Lanfranc, Archbishop of Canterbury 32, 38, 48, 54
language 46

M

Marcher earldoms 20, 22
military service 36, 44
Morcar, Earl of Northumbria 10, 14, 20, 26, 30
murdrum 40

N

nepotism 48
Norman Church 46, 48
Normanisation 30, 38, 48
northern revolt 26, 28

O

Odo, Bishop of Bayeux 38, 50, 54

P

patronage 6, 46
peasants 4, 6, 36, 42
pluralism 48

R

rebellions 8, 10, 26, 28, 30, 32, 52, 54
regents 30, 32, 38, 50
Revolt of the Earls 32
Robert Curthose 52, 54
royal demesne 40

S

sheriffs 4, 38, 40
shield wall 16
shires 4, 38, 44
simony 48
slaves 4, 6, 36, 42
Stamford Bridge, Battle of 14, 16
Stigand, Archbishop of Canterbury 8, 48
submission of the earls 20
succession crisis 10, 12, 14, 54

T

tenants-in-chief 36, 38, 44
thegns 4
towns 6, 42

V

vassals 36
villages 6, 28, 42

W

William I, King of England 10, 12, 16, 20, 26, 28, 30, 32, 36, 38, 40, 48, 50, 52, 54
William II, King of England 54
Witan 4, 12, 14